BE'ER HAGOLAH INSTITUTES

293 Neptune Avenue
Brooklyn, New York 11235

D1501361

I did not come to this country to save myself or to seek positions of personal power," Rabbi Kotler said. "Rather, I am here so that, with your help, we can save our brothers and the centers of Torah learning all over Europe!"

"On the other side of the ocean our brothers are waiting for our help," he continued. "Only you, the Jews of America, are able to help them. Do it now! Save them!"

Rabbi Aharon Kotler

In our generation, thousands of Russian children are landing on American shores each year. And it is now up to us to make the sacrifices.

Be'er Hagolah Institutes was founded ten years ago to combat the forces that were preventing the ideals of Judiasm from reaching the *neshamos* of these innocent children. There are presently over 800 students studying at our school. This number is increasing dramatically each year as a result of the tremendous influx of new Soviet immigrants. Be'er Hagolah's outstanding staff of teachers, guidance counselors, family educators, and professionals offer a full range of educational programs for the students and their parents, as well as social experiences such as family *shabbatonim*, *chavrusa* programs with *bnei yeshivah*, Big Sister-Little Sister, Bais Yaakov programs, summer camping and countless other activities; all geared to introduce and inspire them to Torah living.

"Each generation must answer to a different test. Our generation will have to give testimony regarding what we did for Russian Jews.

Harav Hagaon R'Yaakov Kaminetsky *zt"l*

11/4/91

Dear Mrs. Kaufman, ב"ה

I am currently studying at Bnos Chava seminary in Har Nof, Yerushalayim. Looking back at my years at Beer Hagolah, I have vivid memories of the last few days I spent learning there. Endless nights of crying and worrying that those few days might be my last chance to gather as much knowledge about yiddishkeit as I could. For the next week I was to begin learning in P.S. 127. It is thanks to the endless hours of work of the devoted faculty of Beer Hagolah that I am where I am today. The result of their efforts was that I was able to continue my Jewish education in a Bais Yaakov High School.

I am thankful to the רבונו של עולם that I was fortunate enough to have the guidance in Torah which many of my friends and family lack. I only wish that Beer Hagolah could reach more people like me. Where would I be without you?

Thank You

Sincerely,
Miriam

Heartfelt thanks from a former Be'er Hagolah student.

הַהִסְטוֹרְיָה

The ArtScroll History Series®

Rabbi Nosson Scherman / Rabbi Meir Zlotowitz

General Editors

SILENT

by Miriam Stark Zakon

based on conversations with
RABBI ELIYAHU ESSAS

ЯEVOLUTION

A Torah Network in the Soviet Union

published by

Mesorah Publications, ltd

FIRST EDITION
First Impression . . . November 1992

Published and Distributed by
MESORAH PUBLICATIONS, Ltd.
Brooklyn, New York 11232

Distributed in Israel by
MESORAH MAFITZIM / J. GROSSMAN
Rechov Harav Uziel 117
Jerusalem, Israel

Distributed in Europe by
J. LEHMANN HEBREW BOOKSELLERS
20 Cambridge Terrace
Gateshead, Tyne and Wear
England NE8 1RP

Distributed in Australia & New Zealand by
GOLD'S BOOK & GIFT CO.
36 William Street
Balaclava 3183, Vic., Australia

Distributed in South Africa by
KOLLEL BOOKSHOP
22 Muller Street
Yeoville 2198, South Africa

ARTSCROLL HISTORY SERIES ®
SILENT REVOLUTION
© *Copyright 1992, by* MESORAH PUBLICATIONS, Ltd.
4401 Second Avenue / Brooklyn, N.Y. 11232 / (718) 921-9000

ISBN
0-89906-105-2 (hard cover)
0-89906-106-0 (paperback)

Typography by Compuscribe at ArtScroll Studios, Ltd.

Printed in the United States of America by Noble Book Press Corp.
Bound by Sefercraft, Quality Bookbinders, Ltd. Brooklyn, N.Y.

This book is dedicated
to all the Jews
who grew up in the land
that was once called the Soviet Union.
In Israel, in America, or in your native lands —
as you enjoy the heady taste
of freedom for the first time,
may you speedily learn
the true freedom of the Jewish people:
a life of Torah and mitzvos.

Table of Contents

Prologue:
An Historic Visit

For years, Rabbi Eliyahu Essas had awaited the day when his fondest wish would come true and he would live in the land promised to his forefathers, his home by Divine decree: the Land of Israel. And now that he and his family had finally arrived in Jerusalem, ironically, he was leaving of his own volition, climbing aboard a Boeing 747 that would whisk him half a globe away, to the United States.

What could lure him away, even temporarily, from the beloved land he'd longed for for so many years? His was partially a mission of gratitude — to personally thank those who had fought on his behalf when he was imprisoned behind the Iron Curtain. More important, though, he had come to plead for, and fight for, those who remained behind.

But if the dangers, physical and spiritual, that faced the Jews of the Soviet Union were what preyed on his mind, he soon realized that those fortunate ones who had found freedom in the west were also not immune to the peril ...

◄§ Who Will Teach the Children?

The year was 1979. The problem was — success.

After years of hope and hopelessness, after all the demonstrations, after thousands of words of prayer and Tehillim, the impossible had become commonplace: the Russians were coming! In thousands!

And now that they were here — what in the world would American Jewry do with them?

As any student of American-Jewish history knew, immigrants to "the Goldene Medinah" were usually interested in achieving the American Dream — and achieving it as soon as possible. How many thousands of Jewish men and women, arriving from Torah-true homes in Europe during the great migrations of the 18th century, had cast off their *mitzvos*, throwing their *tefillin* into the churning sea near the Statue of Liberty? What would happen, then, to the thousands of Soviet Jews facing the lure of assimilation, whose background included only the atheistic teachings of the godless regime that had schooled them? What would their future be?

With visionary fearlessness, the *gedolim* of the generation made an historic decision. They would not sit idly by while a generation was lost to Yiddishkeit. They would fight assimilation with the most potent weapon at their disposal — Jewish education.

Like many battles, the fight for the soul of Soviet Jewry began with a declaration of war: a seventy-two word telegram dispatched on September 21, 1979 to some fifty yeshivah principals: "A matter of utmost immediate urgency and deep concern to us compels us to summon some *menahalim* of yeshivos in Brooklyn to a meeting ..." The signatories represented the greatest Torah personalities in America at the time: Rav Moshe Feinstein, זצ"ל, Rav Yaakov Kamenetzky, זצ"ל,

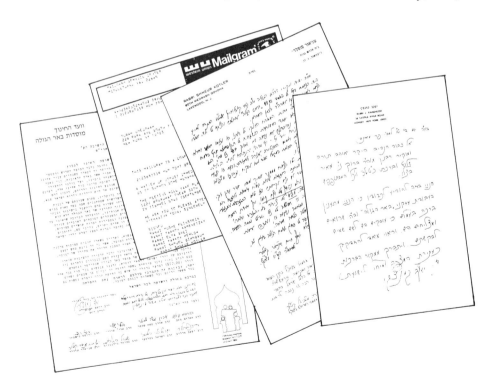

Rav Shneur Kotler, זצ״ל, Rav Elya Svei, Rav Yaakov Perlow, Rav Shmuel Birnbaum, and Rabbi Aaron Schechter.

At the meeting, Rav Yaakov זצ״ל brought up the challenge — what to do with hundreds of Soviet youngsters who needed schools, Jewish schools? "It is a holy obligation ... for every yeshivah to admit the Russians," he declared. Until a permanent solution could be found, he was asking every school to make room for one class of Soviet students. One principal protested that his school was already overcrowded; in fact one of his classes was being taught in a trailer alongside the building. Rav Yaakov said, "Good, rent another trailer." The principal nodded, "I will rent another trailer and put the Russian children into it as the Rosh Yeshivah asked."

"Oh no!" exclaimed Rav Yaakov, "that is not what I meant. Make sure to put the Russian children in a classroom in your building. Take another class and move them into the trailer." To underscore the urgency of the problem, Rav Yaakov refused to call a halt to the meeting to daven *Minchah*.

There was an extra reason to fear for the future of the Soviet Jewish immigrants. For if the Jewish world would not welcome them,·there were others who would ...

◆§ The New Student

The woman walked into the offices of Be'er Hagolah, the school for Soviet Jewish immigrants, one summer's day, and announced, in perfect Lithuanian Yiddish, that she would like to register her child. She herself was trying to live a religious life, had actually fasted on the past *Tishah B'Av*.

The secretary began to fill out the registration forms. "Previous schooling?" she asked.

"St. Sergius Academy."

The room became still, as everyone stared in shocked disbelief. Had this woman, who obviously was trying so hard to be a good Jew, actually allowed her daughter to attend St. Sergius, a Manhattan school run proudly by the Russian Orthodox Church, a hotbed of missionary activity. Why would she do it?

The answer came at once. "First I send my daughter to public school. No good there — drugs, knives. At St. Sergius, when I told the director

I had no money, he said that should not be a reason not to give her a good education. I paid only $50 a month."

A good education. One that included a daily class in religion, lectures on the New Testament, visits to churches, morning prayers where the Jewish students stood with everyone.

The woman looked anxiously around her. Would they refuse her daughter, on the grounds of her enrollment in St. Sergius? "St. Stergius is full of Jewish children," she told them. "It's the Jews fault they are there. Why couldn't I send my child to yeshivah five years ago?"

With the mounting threat of assimilation and missionary activity, the *gedolim* set forth to gather in and educate the youngsters, first in classrooms throughout the New York area; later, they founded the first school for Russian children. The school, Be'er Hagolah opened in 1979 with an enrollment of 400 students. The purpose would be to provide a quality education to Soviet Jewish immigrants.

Thirteen years, and thousands of students, after its founding, Be'er Hagolah, now a "full-service" school with pupils ranging from

Rabbi Essas visiting students at Be'er Hagolah

kindergarten through high school, hosted a very special guest — Rabbi Eliyahu Essas, founder of the *"ba'al teshuvah* movement" in Moscow.

As he gazed at the rows of be-yarmulked young boys who stood in rows to greet him, and as, later, he heard them recite the *aleph-beis*, *Mishnayos*, or words of *Tanach*, he knew he was in the presence of a phenomenon as miraculous in its way as was his own *ba'al teshuvah* movement in the Soviet Union.

ᴇᵨ Her Uncle's Niece

Svetelana was one of those students who brighten a teacher's day: intelligent, interested, eager to learn. She took to religious practice quickly, with an almost startling devotion. Her family was supportive, and soon they, too, had begun observing Shabbos and the laws of *kashrus*.

But though Svetelana's family were happily adjusting to their new homeland, they had not forgotten the relatives they'd left behind, and kept up a regular correspondence. Svetelana's mother wrote to her own father, still in Russia, of the family's religious transformation. Not surprising, her father replied. He could remember his own uncle on his mother's side, a well-known rabbi by the the name of Kagan.

A few more questions, and the secret was revealed. The avid teenager was none other than the great-niece of the Chofetz Chaim.

ᴇᵨ Yiddishe Nachas

It was a wedding invitation like many others: Two sets of parents who would be honoured with your presence at the marriage of their children Shifra to Hershel.

As in any wedding, there was much *"Yiddishe nachas"* to be reaped: parents, relatives, friends. But, in this case, there was one big difference: the greatest *"nachas"* came to the Rav who'd been honored as *mesader kiddushin*: Rav Avrohom Pam. For though Rav Pam hardly knew the *choson* and *kallah*, he knew something else: the *kallah* was a graduate of Be'er Hagolah, the institution he'd worked so hard to create. This newest *bayis ne'eman b'Yisrael* would have been an impossible dream, had not he and so many others fought to build that dream.

Rav Schneur Kotler ל״צז, too, merited great *"nachas"* before his untimely death. One of the last groups that he met with, when he was

Rav Avrohom Pam with Be'er Hagolah students

already terribly ill and confined to bed, was a delegation of youngsters from Be'er Hagolah. After the boys had shyly answered his questions in Gemara, Rav Kotler זצ"ל laboriously sat up and smiled. "When we began, we never thought it was possible that we would see such a thing. We had to do our job, but we never really believed we would see such success," he said.

◄§ An Historic Visit

During his 1986 visit, Rabbi Essas was so moved by his experience in the yeshivah that he cancelled all further appointments for his busy day, preferring to spend his time with the children. Children out of godless Russia; children snatched from the hands of missionaries; children teaching parents to say their first *berachah;* children fighting family pressure for the right to live as Torah Jews.

Children, always children, creating their own silent revolution.

Foreword

When I was first approached by the editors of ArtScroll with the suggestion that I write my autobiography, my reaction was strong and definite: I would refuse. I had never viewed myself as someone whose biography was of interest to anyone other than my family and close friends. In addition, I felt that at my relatively young age, it would be inappropriate to write an autobiography.

But I found it difficult to come out with a quick and definite refusal. After all, these were the editors of ArtScroll, the respected publishing house whose books were so precious to me and my *talmidim* during those dark days in the Soviet Union when we were cut off from contact with the outside world, when our learning had to come almost solely from within ourselves.

How could I possibly say no to them?

As I formulated a polite way to reply in the negative, I began to gain a different perspective on their proposal. Perhaps what they wanted was not merely my autobiography; perhaps they wanted the story of a remarkable chapter in Jewish history, one which few people were familiar with. Here was a group of people who began with an almost complete lack of Torah knowledge and yet created a Torah community and ultimately lived full Jewish lives — all under the most adverse of circumstances. This, then, was a phenomenon worth chronicling.

The editors of ArtScroll and I finally agreed that I would discuss the history and recount the tales of this remarkable group with a writer of their choice. I was happy to share the story with my brethren throughout the world. It is, after all, a part of our common history — for we are, ultimately, one family, one people.

What followed was a series of conversations with Mrs. Miriam Zakon. I am thankful to Miriam for being a faithful listener as well as a creative writer. Her book is now presented to the reader: a series of unusual tales of a very unusual movement.

I want to express my deepest thanks to several individuals who have had a marked impact upon my life. To my dear parents, Tzvi Hirsch and Sonya Essas, for instilling in me the deep and strong feeling of belonging to my people and to my land. These views were transmitted to me during the darkest days of the Soviet regime, under the terrifying rule of Stalin.

Their efforts lie at the root of all my later accomplishments. To my father, too, my deepest appreciation for his ten years of tireless efforts to free me from the Soviet Union.

To my wife, Anya, and my children Yosef, Esther, and David, for their patience and understanding — even in their earliest years — during the countless hours, the *Shabbos* afternoons, and the *Pesach sedarim* that I spent away from our home.

The revolution that this book recounts took place in an atmosphere created by dozens of Jewish organizations and groups and thousands of people: an atmosphere of Jewish solidarity. Obviously, I cannot mention all of them — the list would be much longer than this book! — but I must point out a few whose efforts were connected with my life personally, or whose achievements were too great to pass by and whose names do not appear in the stories of this book. To Nechemiah Levanon, R' Meir Kahane z"l, Isi J. Liebler, R' Dovid Hill, Hans Bachrach, Zeesy Schnur, Ruth Bloch, Rita Ekker, and Myrna Shinbaum who, together with thousands of people in Israel, the United States, Canada, Great Britain, Australia, Denmark and Switzerland, were organizing, pushing, moving demonstrating, writing letters, lobbying, and praying — my fervent thanks.

But solidarity was not only felt in the west. Hundreds of Jews in the Soviet Union, many of whom did not join our Torah community, still helped us to begin, and succeed in, our revolution, by helping, encouraging, publicizing, bringing in materials. Many of them were my comrades in our struggle for *aliyah*. To mention just a few: Pavel Abramovich, Vladimir Prestin, Alexander Voronel, Natan Scharansky, Vladimir Lazaris, and Yuli Kosharovsky.

And finally, my acknowledgment to my students, my beloved *talmidim*. Some of them are the heroes in the stories of this book. Others are not mentioned, only because their stories did not fit into the book's format. And many of their lives deserve books unto themselves.

This book is not meant to be a substitute for historical research or a fundamental treatise about an almost unimaginable phenomenon: the rebirth of Jewish life under the relentless pressure of a mighty tyranny. This book is meant to give the reader a feeling, a sense of what this revolution meant, how it came to be, and how it could succeed under such incredibly difficult circumstances. It is my fervent hope that it inspire Jews throughout the world, living under many different political and economic situations, with the understanding that *mesiras nefesh*, sacrifice and dedication for the Jewish people, can work miracles — and can bring about revolutions.

Eliyahu Essas

Introduction

Most people know at least a little about the Russian Revolution, the 1917 revolt that brought Lenin and his Bolsheviks into power. Those with more than a passing familiarity with the era are aware that there were actually two Russian revolutions: the February Revolution, which marked the end of the czarist regime, and the October Revolution, when the Bolsheviks triumphed and the Communist era began.

But only a small number have ever heard of still another revolution that took place after six decades of Communist rule. It was a quiet affair, as revolutions go: no guns, no tanks, no press releases or media coverage. By revolutionary standards, it was tiny, encompassing, at its height, several hundred people. But each person is an entire world, the Sages say — and who can gauge the spiritual impact of hundreds of Jews rediscovering Torah in a totalitarian state dedicated to destroying all religious belief in its countrymen?

This book tells the story of that revolution.

Rabbi Eliyahu Essas:
A Short Biography

The air was balmy on the Sunday in June when Tzvi Hirsch Essas, a native of the city of Yurbark in Lithuania, set out from Kovno on a one-day trip with his fiancee, Sonya Blank. They were traveling to Telz, Sonya's hometown, to visit her family there. The year was 1941.

The train made its smoky way through the Lithuanian countryside, chugging ever-closer to its destination. Suddenly, the pastoral peace was shattered. Curious passengers craned their necks to see what was making that dreadful noise, to catch a glimpse of what was going on.

What was going on was war — Blitzkrieg, "lightning war," as the Nazi Germans liked to call it. Wave after wave of planes dropped their deadly loads; platoons of soldiers marched relentlessly ahead, carrying with them tons of artillery. Like an untamed, vicious beast, the Nazis had turned upon their erstwhile friends, the Communists — and the battleground was Lithuania.

"Go east! Go east!" Frightened soldiers told the train's crew. "Do not return to Lithuania! Go east, to Russia. To safety!" The train, exiled from its homeland, raced eastward, fleeing the merciless bombers. Eventually,

Tzvi Hirsch and Sonya Essas, now living in Jerusalem.

the passengers, now refugees, were settled in the barren wastes of Samarkand, the Central Asian portion of the U.S.S.R.

Tzvi Hirsch Essas' day trip lasted over three years, until the war's end. When peace finally came to Lithuania, he and Sonya, now a married couple, refused to return to their hometowns. Who should they return to? Sonya's father, a respected layman in Telz, had gone to his death along with most of the students of the famed city's *yeshivah*. Virtually all of their other relatives had perished in the Holocaust, with the enthusiastic acquiescence of their Lithuanian neighbors.

The Essas family, like many other Lithuanian Jews who had survived the war, chose instead to settle in the city of Vilnius [Vilna]. There they began the difficult task of rebuilding their lives under the frightening shadow of Stalin's rule.

Like most of his friends, their son, Ilya, grew up with a strong feeling for his Jewish heritage. His neighbors, with their anti-Semitic taunts, would not let him forget he was a Jew. His government, with the word "Yevrei" stamped on the fifth line of his identity card, would not let him forget he was a Jew. And his parents, who would meet on the Soviet Independence Day to speak quietly of Israel and Zionism, did everything in their power — limited though it was in the Stalinist regime — to inculcate within their son a love for his people: to make sure he would not forget he was a Jew.

But Jewish identity is not observance. Pride in a heritage is no substitute for Torah knowledge — forbidden knowledge, in the Soviet Union. The penalty for teaching a youngster religion was three years in prison. Few were willing to risk the threat of the *gulag,* the dreaded labor camps where so many perished. Thus Ilya Essas, scion of generations of *talmidei chachamim* and pious *ba'alei batim,* brilliant student at the University in Vilnius, knew almost nothing of his people's history and of their Torah.

The years passed. As a graduate student in mathematics, Essas was allowed use of the Vilnius Academy library. Among the stacks of abstruse mathematical tomes he found a hidden treasure: worn copies of Graetz's *History of the Jews,* Herzl's *Judenstaadt,* and a Jewish encyclopedia. They were there in the library for the purpose of anti-Zionist research, the bemused student guessed. But why on earth were they not in the classified stacks, where such dangerous materials were usually stored?

This was the first of several startling examples of *hashgachah pratis* (Divine intervention) in the young student's life. Instead of reading his math books, Essas pored over the forbidden words, eagerly amassing knowledge on subjects he had heretofore never dreamed existed. Though he didn't learn too much from his limited resources, he did glean two important facts. He realized that he knew nothing about his traditions and his people. And he realized that he had to know more.

Essas married Anya Sheinin in 1970 and the young couple moved to Moscow, Anya's hometown. Essas, still searching blindly for knowledge of things Jewish, quickly connected up with the most visible — indeed, possibly the only — Jewish presence in the capital: the refuseniks.

The Six Day War had marked a watershed in the history of Soviet Jewry. Despite the constant barrage of anti-Israel propaganda disseminated by the government, the Jews of the Soviet Union were electrified by word of Israel's extraordinary victory. Not long afterwards a few foolhardy souls approached the OVIR (Visa Application and Registration) office in Moscow with an outlandish request: They wanted to leave the "Worker's Paradise," permanently. They wanted to go to their homeland — Israel. The outrageous request was, naturally, turned down, and a new word entered the vocabulary of dictatorships: refusenik.

A refusenik remembered: Tzvi Hirsch Essas demands his son's freedom, Philadelphia, 1978.

The Essases swiftly became a part of this community, taking part in its rites and rituals: the Saturday afternoon meetings on Archipov Street, next to the Moscow Synagogue; the illegal talks with foreign correspondents; the Hebrew lessons; the countless petitions and *samizdats*, underground newsletters. In 1973, when Essas' petition to leave was officially denied on the grounds that his wife, Anya, had spent one year working in the missile industry (a year that would ultimately cost them thirteen years of refusal), he found himself, like his friends, a full-fledged refusenik.

Though he was busy with refusenik activities, his life was taking a sharply different turn. Learning of Essas' fascination with Jewish books, Hebrew teacher and refusenik Josif Begun sent him to the man who would be his first "rebbe," Lev Gurevich, a self-styled "religious atheist" who had never lost the love for learning inculcated into him in his years as a youthful student in the *yeshivah* of Volozhin. Essas, enthralled, discovered the world of Torah learning — *Tanach, Mishnah, Gemara, Rishonim* and *Acharonim. This* was no Jewish encyclopedia! But, unlike his *"rebbe,"* Essas soon realized that learning was empty unless accompanied by *mitzvah* observance. Five years after he had come across his first Jewish books, Eliyahu Essas had become an observant Jew.

But the revolution that took place in his own life was merely a beginning. With the guidance of Hashem, Essas had found an eternal truth; now, his was the responsibility to teach others.

What can be termed, for lack of a better word, a Torah network, began in a small living room with fifteen mildly curious young men. Curiosity turned to fascination; fascination, to commitment. Within months, his students, still learning, became teachers themselves, spreading words of Torah to people hungry for them. In the years that followed, the network grew: Zev and Carmela Raiz in Vilna, Grisha Wasserman in Leningrad, Valery Lemelman in Odessa — all began to give *shiurim*. A most unlikely *"kehillah"* formed, a *kehillah* separated by thousands of kilometers, with its own methods of distributing kosher food, teaching its children, protecting its members, and staying out of KGB notice.

What follows are tales of this *"kehillah"*: the Communist society whose restrictions shaped it, the people who dedicated their lives to it, the sacrifices that helped it to grow. All the stories are true. Occasionally, names have been changed or surnames left out at the request of those involved.

A personal note: It has been almost four years since I met with Rabbi Essas in his office in downtown Jerusalem in order to begin this book. It is an indication of the swiftness of world events today that when I first suggested a biography of Rabbi Essas to ArtScroll/Mesorah Publications, the Soviet Union was the second greatest power on the globe, *perestroika* and *glasnost* were just two more unpronounceable Russian words, and the possibility of a mass migration of Soviet Jews an unspeakable dream.

When I first met Rabbi Essas, in the home of Rabbi Mordechai Neustadt, director of Agudath Israel of America's Vaad L'Hatzolas Nidchei Yisrael, I was struck by the man's humility, intelligence, and sincere compassion for his fellows. Since that evening I have met with him many, many times, and each time I have been struck anew by his selfless dedication. Writing a book is hard drudgery, arduous labor — and with all that, about as satisfying an enterprise as a person could wish for. When, in addition, it becomes an opportunity for gaining incredible inspiration from a truly unique individual, it is indeed a privilege. For that inspiration I thank Rabbi Essas.

Sivan 5752   M.Z.

CHAPTER 1

Mother Russia and Father Stalin: Parents of a Generation

There is a dangerous tendency on the part of chroniclers to wax enthusiastic about movements and disregard one important fact: Movements are composed, after all, of people. And people have pasts. People begin their lives, not as movers and shakers, not as leaders or visionaries or martyrs to a cause; people begin their lives as children.

Most of the characters who were to play a major role in what became known as the Soviet ba'al teshuvah movement were children growing up under the watchful eye of two frightening parents: Mother Russia and Father Stalin.

◈ Life in the Courtyard

Rabbi Eliyahu Essas vividly remembers his own experiences as a youth growing up in Lithuania. He shared a courtyard with two Jewish families, four Poles, one Lithuanian and two Russians. "I got it from all sides," he says wryly.

"An old Polish woman, Pani Maria, used to sit, bedridden, by her window. Every morning when I left the courtyard, and every evening upon my return, I was greeted by her words. 'Here comes the dirty Jew. The Poles will come and kill you.' "

Later, when her neighbors finally made her realize that the Poles no longer ruled Lithuania, Pani Maria changed her tune. "The Russians will finish the job the Poles started. Then Americans will come and hang you on a tree."

Ten-year-old Ilya Essas in Soviet school uniform, Vilnius, 1956.

Such were the daily benedictions that greeted five-year-old Ilya.

At six, Ilya was left with his neighbor, Anastasia, for a short while. The friendly woman read the child stories for a while; when that pursuit palled, she led him to her small living room and pointed to a portrait hung proudly over the mantel. "Remember, this is our god on earth," she said to the curious child, as she pointed to the picture hanging on the wall. The youngster stared at the serious, mustached face with the oddly piercing eyes that stood before him: Marshal Stalin.

She then led the youngster into her own room. Carefully closing the door, she lifted a curtain and revealed a hidden recess. Inside was the type of icon that had once graced every Russian Orthodox home.

"And this," she said, her voice barely above a whisper, "this is our Father in heaven."

It was, remembers Rabbi Essas, his first lesson in theology.

> *The anti-Semitism was there, palpable, and evil as a cancer. And yet it served its purpose: Not for the first time, it was the hatred borne by the non-Jew that was the means of keeping the Jew aware of his heritage.*
>
> *Anti-Semitism was, in one dimension, G-d's secret gift to the Jews, the means of keeping their religion alive. For in the Soviet Union of Josef Stalin, there was no other way...*

⋑ Jewish Education: Not at Any Price

The first day of school. The youngsters file into the classroom, a little tense, a little excited, wondering what lies in store for them.

They soon find out. The teacher stares sternly at them, and barks out a question:

"Who believes in G-d?" she asks.

Some of the children, still not schooled in the ways of the Communist state, hesitantly lift their hands.

Teacher's voice grows gentle, though her eyes are still hard. "Now, children," she says quietly, "I want all of you to close your eyes tight and pray as hard as you can to G-d for something very, very good."

Eyes close shut in intense concentration. The children's brows grow wrinkled; some sway back and forth. A young Jewish child, perhaps remembering some words of his ancient grandmother, whispers "*Shema Yisrael.*"

"Open your eyes, children."

The desks are bare.

Teacher smiles again. "Now, children, close your eyes very tight and ask the glorious Communist state to give you something very, very good."

The silence in the room is broken by a slight rustling. At the teacher's signal, the eyes are opened. The youngsters, delighted, gaze at the small mound of candies piled upon each desk.

"There is no G-d, children. He does not answer your prayers. Only the state will answer your prayers."

The lesson was over. And it was well learned.

Children growing up under Father Stalin learned other lessons, and learned them quickly.

The Shadow of Fear

A Russian *ba'al teshuvah* now living in Jerusalem remembers:

Like all children, we used to tell jokes. Here are two that we used to share — very quietly.

Once, Marshal Stalin lost his pipe. He called in the head of the NKVD and demanded that the thief be apprehended and punished. The next day, Stalin found the pipe lying in a corner. He contacted the NKVD chief and told him he could drop the investigation.

"But Sir," the man protested, "twelve people have already confessed!"

And this one: Four men are sitting in a jail cell in one of Stalin's labor camps. Suddenly, a new prisoner is thrown in. The men turn to him.

"How long are you in for?"

"Twenty-five years."

"And what did you do?"

"Nothing. Absolutely nothing."

"Liar! For doing nothing — you only get ten years!"

If any and all religious observance was frowned upon by the authorities, Judaism came in for special attention.

ᴥᔆ Sasha's Tale: Beginnings

Sasha is a religious Jew living in Jerusalem. He keeps *Shabbos*, studies Torah and observes the *mitzvos* to the best of his ability.

It wasn't always like that.

Sasha was seven years old. He never gave much thought to his nationality. If pressed, he would have said he was a Russian, but it didn't really matter, did it?

It did.

He was walking to school when a burly twelve-year-old student, a classmate of his brother's, suddenly appeared, barring the way. "Tell me what nationality you are," he demanded.

Sasha thought for a few moments. "Russian," he answered, not really comprehending the reason for the interrogation.

"Tell me what nationality you are," the twelve-year-old demanded again.

Sasha looked up at him, his clear blue eyes puzzled. What did this kid want, anyway?

Suddenly, the bigger boy raised his fist and pounded Sasha in the face.

As the blood trickled out of his nose and jaw, Sasha heard the bully's words, as if in a dream: "You're a Zhid, Zhid, Zhid."

"If parents forget to tell their children they are Jewish," Sasha says today, a touch of irony in his tone, "there will be a *goy* there to remind him."

For youngsters who would one day take the surprising path to their Jewish heritage, anti-Semitism was a fact of life, as was the shadow of a malevolent dictator. One further factor seems to have influenced these young men and women: the primitivism of their non-Jewish neighbors.

⊰ The People in the Neighborhood

Rabbi Essas remembers: The Russians in our neighborhood got paid every two weeks. They would then take their money and get drunk for three days. For ten days they would be sober and then. . . payday! During those three days of horror in our courtyard, we were always on the alert and tried to hide from our neighbors. But we weren't their only victims; I remember how one drunken Communist once took a knife and tried to kill his equally drunken father, who defended himself by hitting his son over the head with a chair. Alexei the policeman, another courtyard resident, would take his pistol home sometimes and threaten his own family and others. When we'd spend a Lithuanian holiday at a resort, we always knew that the next day we'd see the funerals of those *goyim* who had drunkenly entered the sea, usually fully dressed, and drowned.

When you were seven years old and growing up in the Soviet Union, the anti-Semitism would be clean, brisk and hard: a rap in the face, a kick in the back. When you were seventeen, things had become more subtle.

⊰ Higher Education, Greater Hatred

Because of his "straight A" high school marks, Ilya Essas, Jew though he was, had a good shot at getting into University. He needed those straight A's; otherwise, he'd have been subjected to five entrance exams, each of which was designed to weed out uppity Jewish students such as he. As it was, he had to pass only one test.

He entered the examiner's bare office braced for the ordeal. He knew it wouldn't be easy: Lithuanians used to hand out C's and D's routinely to Jewish students, ensuring their rejection. Still, with his background, they wouldn't dare hand out such a mark unless they could make it stick.

The test was oral — a more objective written test wouldn't do for him. Instead of the usual two to three hours of mathematics problems, he was subjected to five hours of intensive questioning. The problems were grueling: Essas had never seen their like before. Every once in a while, his Lithuanian tester would politely mention that he was getting everything wrong and was heading for a grade of "F."

When his five hours were up, Ilya Essas had come through with a

Ilya Essas, University graduate, 1969.

grade of A minus. "He got his minus, but I got into University," Rabbi Essas laughs.

Later, at home, Essas searched in vain through his high school and college texts for the problems he'd been asked. He finally did find them — in a mathematics competition book designed for an "Olympiad" of professional mathematicians!

Some years later, Assistant Professor Ilya Essas found evidence as to how effective such stratagems for keeping Jews out of higher education were. As head of the curriculum department in Moscow Medical School, he had access to school documents being sent to the Ministry of Education as part of an annual report. Among the items of note was a breakdown of students by nationality. Thirty nationalities, including Jewish, appeared on the list. Next to each listing was a number indicating what percentage of the student body belonged to each nationality. Only one number was circled in heavy red ink: Jewish, 4%. In Moscow's other two medical schools, the percentage of Jews was 0 and 1%; Moscow's Jews make up 7% of the total population. Thus, 4% was already dangerously high, and warranted special notice!

Anti-Semitism wasn't confined to the classroom and the campus; it was everywhere.

⤳ In the Kolchoz

One of the most horrifying chapters of the Stalin era was the forced collectivization of farmers in the 1930s, an economic strategy that led to as many as fifteen million deaths by famine in what had been one of the most fertile areas of Europe. The collective farms, *kolchozes* as they were called, became agricultural disaster areas, with demoralized farmers hardly doing any work.

In order to assist the farmers, University students were sent to work on the farms. In the early '70s, one young Jewish student found himself on a mandatory program designed to help out the beleaguered *kolchozniks*. As the truck pulled out of the University's yard, heading for a Lithuanian *kolchoz*, the young student noticed, with some trepidation, that he was the only Jew in the group of twenty-five students.

All went well until Sunday, when his fellow students, having drunk all of the *samogon* (homemade vodka) that they could lay their hands on, began to hurl those timeworn epithets at him, the lone Jew. A quarrel began, with three schools of thought. The first, and most vocal, insisted that the Jew be killed immediately. The second group suggested that they wait for two or three days, to see how he would behave. The third, made up of only one or two more timid souls, worried that the affair would get them in trouble.

As the argument grew heated, someone began to sharpen a knife.

The student tried not to panic. Escape was impossible, not in this lonely stable out in the middle of nowhere that was serving as a dormitory. It was a cold and rainy night and not a soul was about. Perhaps, he thought, he hoped, that like so many drunken *goyim* that he'd seen over the years, they would begin to fight each other and forget about him. Perhaps. . .

Suddenly, the roar of a jeep interrupted the drunken shouts. The group's supervisor had returned from a visit to the nearest town. The sight of him sobered up the students, who quickly dispersed.

And Ilya Essas, the Jewish student, had learned his lesson once again In Soviet Russia, a Jew remains a Jew.

> *Anti-Semitism in the schools. Anti-Semitism on the farms. And, anti-Semitism in that third great institution of the socialist state — the army. Again, a ba'al-teshuvah-to-be learned that even if he didn't know much about his Jewishness, others did.*

⋍§ The Specter of the Army

Ilya Essas chose to spend his five years in Vilnius University studying mathematics. As he had done in high school, Essas excelled in his studies, graduating at the very top of his class.

Normally about ten percent of a graduating class were drafted into the Soviet army. The rest of the class, under the Soviet system, were

Left: Ilya Essas, at presentation of MA thesis in mathematics, answers a tough question hurled at him by an anti-Semitic professor. The thesis got an A+, but that couldn't save him from the draft.

Right: Riga army base, 1968: Private Ilya Essas on reserve duty. Standing to his right is Corporal Oleinik, a notorious Ukranian anti-Semite. Oleinik is smiling, having just received a bribe from Essas in exchange for granting him a few hours' leave so that he can visit his parents, visiting in Riga. This photo would normally have been confiscated upon emigration, but was smuggled out by R' Essas' father.

forced to spend the next three years in jobs assigned to them by the state. Most of these, naturally, were located in frigid and distant parts of the Union, where qualified workers were hard to come by. Still, as one of the top three graduates of his class, student Essas had the good fortune to be able to choose his work assignment.

Or so he thought.

Essas entered the room where his professors were sitting waiting for him. The men were effusive in their praise for his high marks. "The Minister of Defense himself has recognized your accomplishment, Comrade Essas. Such talent is needed in the highest circles — the military."

Drafted. He was being drafted.

The military was no new phenomenon to Ilya Essas. As part of his college requirements, every student was required to give one day per week, and an additional two months at the end of college, to the army. Essas vividly remembers his stint during the summer of 1968, not long after the famed "Prague Spring":

"My brigade, based in a Riga military base, was in communications, trained to serve large armies in the Baltic area. In the middle of July, more than one month before the Soviet Union's invasion of Czechoslovakia, the army sent more than 1,000 tanks from the Urals and the Baltic to Poland and Czechoslovakia. In my capacity as communications technician I myself overheard the head of military intelligence for the area telling a colleague: 'In two or three weeks we'll be in Prague.' This was the 'unplanned, spontaneous' invasion the Soviets would speak of!

"Of the three battalions in Riga, two went on to Czechoslovakia, and mine was left behind. My company was composed mainly of Lithuanians, with a handful of Jews, and some Russian officers. It was the same old story: Some sixty Lithuanian soldiers, all students like myself, were bored, so they decided to kill one or two Jews, just to keep life interesting. They drew lots to decide on their victims. It was eight Jewish students versus these Lithuanians, with the Russians keeping out of things.

"We could sense their plotting. The tension was tremendous. We knew it would happen, but when? And how? It would be some kind of accident, that was certain. A fire in the barracks? A shooting accident?

"Time was passing. Our stint was coming to an end. If anything would happen, it would be soon. Suddenly, early one morning, a Lithuanian sentry kicked the door open and announced the news. He'd been listening to the BBC — the Soviet Union had invaded Prague!

"The hatred suddenly disappeared. The Lithuanians, whose sympathies were totally with the Czechs, focused all of their loathing on the Russians. We had a common enemy: Suddenly, we were allies against the Russian colonialists.

"It was my last week in the army, and I had been spared. It was August 21, 1968: my own personal Purim!"

The scenes of his military service were clear in the mind of the young student, now faced with the prospect of twenty-five years of servitude. And Essas had a second compelling reason for avoiding military service. At the time, the first stirrings of Zionism had begun within him, and emigration was a real possibility. Like every other Soviet Jew, he knew that a military career, no matter how short, sounded a death knell to hopes of an emigration visa. And Essas had no intention of becoming a refusenik.

Thus, this unexpected development was nothing short of disaster.

Essas looked at the smiling faces of his professors as they sat before him. He knew what they were thinking: The plum positions shall not go to the Jews. Let the Lithuanians enjoy it; let the Jew rot in the army.

He protested the assignment. As a top student he was entitled to choose his assignment. Yes, they replied, you may choose your position in the civilian world — but the army has chosen you.

He left the office and quickly raced to the head of the University's military department, Colonel Wolf Vilensky, himself a Jew. A World War II hero, bearer of the Motherland's highest decoration, the Gold Star, Vilensky turned out to be, alas, another Jew who had turned his back on his brethren. He had, in fact, hatched the plot together with the University director. To Essas' complaints he responded: "Go and prove you're a good Soviet citizen."

Ilya Essas refused to accept defeat.

He had only one more day before all assignments were finalized. He dashed off to a local Jewish doctor. A member of the Lithuanian-Jewish intelligentsia, Dr. Aronin had trained under the foremost physicians of France and Switzerland, in the days when Lithuania had been a free, independent country. He had always proved himself a friend to Jews in need and this was no exception. He took one look at a minor, temporary skin problem that Ilya had, and immediately gave him an official notice stating that Ilya Essas was suffering from a major skin disease that needed medical treatment.

The next day, to the chagrin of the smiling professors, Essas walked in with his doctor's statement. Because the note meant delay, and because assignments were to be completed that very day, Essas could no longer be considered for the army.

Another Jew had been saved, for a fate that he could not have dreamed of.

CHAPTER 2

That Which Endured

To write that the Soviet system had succeeded in obliterating all traces of observance from the life of its Jews would not be quite accurate. Some institutions remained. Like any other Torah center, Moscow in Khrushchev's time, and beyond, could boast of — would you believe — both a shul and a yeshivah!

◄§ Our Esteemed President

The Moscow Main Synagogue, one of the two *shuls* remaining in what had once been a city with a large, vibrant Jewish community, was the last bastion of *Yiddishkeit* in the Soviet Union. And what a bastion it was! Most of the thirty or forty "regulars" were elderly Jews. Many were crotchety; some were, quite frankly, eccentric.

And none was more eccentric than the synagogue's esteemed president, Efraim Kaploun.

Kaploun's eating habits already set him apart from the realm of ordinary mortals. Every day, three times daily, Kaploun would sit down to his meal. In one hand he held his glass of vodka; in the other, a thick, green scallion. He'd place the scallion down on the table, greedily fork up a piece of meat (unfortunately, not kosher), wash it down with vodka and another bite of scallion. This exclusive diet of vodka, meat and scallions had, by the 1970s, turned his nose a bright shade of blue. With his heavy, lumbering gait, his blue nose, and his omnipresent walking stick, he looked very much what he was: a dignified drunkard.

As head of the synagogue's *dvadzatka*, board of directors, Kaploun had access to many lucrative sources of income. The synagogue would sell *matzah* every year at two rubles per kilo. With an average yearly sale of 200,000 pounds, the *dvadzatka* pocketed (after bribes to appropriate officials) some 100,000 rubles. (The average Soviet worker earned two hundred rubles per month.) Then there was the sale of *kaddish*, the sale of wine, even the sale of *talleisim* and *tzitzis* donated by visiting foreigners to elderly Soviet Jews!

With such high stakes, it was inevitable that there would be challenges to Kaploun's leadership. Here the importance of his walking stick became pronounced. One morning, for instance, the previous president of the synagogue staged a "coup," with some backers facing Kaploun and demanding his resignation.

Kaploun acted swiftly. He cut the phone wires and barred himself in his office. His challenger immediately broke down the door, lifted the half-full vodka glass from Kaploun's desk, and deliberately threw it into his face. Ignoring the blood pouring down from the scratches (later he was to laugh that "vodka is the best disinfectant"), Kaploun picked up his walking stick and brought it down sharply upon his opponent. The seventy-year-old president of the synagogue then lifted up the sixty-eight-year-old ex-president of the synagogue and sent him soaring out the door. He flew through the air and landed, in a heap, upon the *bimah*.

Such was the Jewish leadership sanctioned by the Communist regime.

Where there is a shul, there's a rabbi . . . of sorts . . .

ᴇ§ The Ersatz Rabbi

The year was 1972. The problem was the Jews. America's Secretary of State, Henry Kissinger, was to visit Moscow as part of his policy of detente. All Moscow was to get a refurbishing for the occasion.

But Kissinger, unfortunately, was a Jew. He'd probably be interested in Jewish life in the Soviet Union. And what did they have to show him?

For the Soviet Union, a great industrial state, shortage of an item was no problem: What was missing would be manufactured. And in the Soviet Union, a Union of Socialist Republics, what was manufactured would not be, well, of the finest quality.

And so came about the ersatz Chief Rabbi.

Secretary of State Kissinger was introduced to the Chief Rabbi of Moscow by his Soviet counterpart, Andrei Gromyko. A fine-looking man, this Rabbi Fishman, distinguished, with his white beard and erect carriage.

Mrs. Gromyko, also introduced to the Chief Rabbi, smiled graciously and inclined her head slightly. Yet as he walked away, she looked back at him, a slight frown playing on her face. Though this was her first meeting with him, she knew she had seen that face before. A politician, and his spouse, must have a good memory for such things. Where had she seen that man before?

She made an effort of memory. Surely it had something to do with the theater. Yes! The amateur theater of the automotive factory, the one she was patron over. No, impossible. The Chief Rabbi of Moscow — was the cloakroom attendant in the theater?

Impossible, but true.

In 1955, in a short period of liberalization after Stalin's death, the Soviet Union had graciously permitted the opening of a *yeshivah*. Though it was closed by Khrushchev after about six years, it did manage to train several *shochtim* who would later take an important place in the remnant of Soviet Jewish life. And among its students — though he never graduated — was one Yakov Fishman.

With the closing of the *yeshivah*, Fishman was given a vague, noncommittal reference, and wound up trying to lead the Jewish community in faraway Perm. When he discovered that communal work was not for him, he returned to Moscow and took a job in the cloakroom of an automobile plant, there to quietly while away the hours until duty called.

When faced with the problem of producing a rabbi, the authorities turned to the now-defunct *yeshivah*. But out of thirty or so men who had studied there, it was difficult to find one who fit the bill. They needed someone, first and foremost, with presence, bearing, and a long beard. Any real scholar was considered untrustworthy; besides, most would not have considered such a position, because of the inevitable collaboration with the KGB that it would entail.

Yakov Fishman. Not too bright. Actually a complete ignoramus. Long beard. Dignified with his spectacles and his pure, high brow, unwrinkled by deep thought. And, most important, prepared to collaborate fully and enthusiastically with the authorities.

The cloakroom attendant's day had arrived. He had become a Chief Rabbi.

But some pockets of sacrifice and greatness did survive, even amidst the low comedy and high tragedy of Soviet Judaism. The Jewish spirit, in possibly its more pure form, could be found in many of its elderly men and women, just as it was stirring, still unnoticed, among some numbers of young people.

≈§ Reb Shalom Tovbin

The Moscow synagogue, though liberally populated by a sprinkling of rowdies, toughs, oddballs, and KGB informers, also had its pious, humble, *Jewish* Jews.

Shalom Tovbin, for instance. Reb Shalom taught the *Gemara shiur* every day after *Shacharis* and between *Minchah* and *Ma'ariv*. He would sit at the head of a large table, the *"Gemara tish,"* with ten to fifteen elderly men seated around him. A remarkable phenomenon, this *"tish"*: possibly the only place left in the Soviet Union where *Gemara* was still being taught.

Who was this elderly Reb Shalom? He had learned in Brisk before the First World War. When nine-year-old Yoshe Ber Soloveitchik needed someone to review his *Gemara* lessons, it was this young *bochur*, Reb Shalom, who was chosen by his father for the job. Now, after close to a lifetime spent in Communist Russia, he still taught *Gemara* to his fellow Jews.

On the last day of his life, *Rosh Chodesh Cheshvan* 5738, Reb Shalom proclaimed during *Hallel*, in a voice so loud that it drew the attention of everyone in the room, *"lo hamaysim y'hallelu kah*: The dead shall not praise the L-rd."

After prayers he slowly rose and with all the difficulty of his eighty-five years of life, walked with his assistant, Reb Avrom Miller, out of the synagogue. Suddenly he halted, gripped his chest. He turned to Reb Avrom and whispered to him: "Only, keep the *tish*."

With those words, he collapsed and died.

≈§ The Silent Yom Kippur

Reb Avrom Miller, who took over the *shiur*, was another example of this older generation. Born in Dvinsk, he could remember his mother going to the extraordinary Rogatchover Gaon, the Rav of the town, with her day-to-day *sh'eilos*. At fourteen he was sent to learn at the *yeshivah*

R' Avrom Miller in the Moscow Synagogue.

of Rav Yisrael Meir HaCohen Kagan. To the end of his days, Reb Avrom would speak of "my rebbe, the Chafetz Chaim."

After the Revolution, Reb Avrom became a state-sanctioned itinerant peddler, traveling from one small townlet to the next with his wares, keeping the *mitzvos* as best he could.

Once, in those fear-filled 1930s, Reb Avrom found himself in the city of Kostroma, a regional capital. Alone, friendless — on *erev Yom Kippur*. Where could he go? Would he be able to *daven* with a *minyan*? It appeared not.

As he wandered through the city's deserted streets, he noticed a man staring at him; staring, particularly at the cap which covered his head. The man looked at him pointedly, and then, without a word, raised his eyebrows, nodded his head ever so slightly, and walked off. In the Stalin era, the message was clear: Follow me.

A fellow Jew? An agent of the ubiquitous NKVD, the secret police, looking for a new recruit for Siberia? An angel of G-d?

Reb Avrom hesitated for just one moment, and then followed the man through street after winding street. Not long before sunset they reached their ultimate destination, a wooden house at the city's outskirts. The strange man opened the door and entered. Reb Avrom, with a silent prayer on his lips, followed.

Inside, he found ten or twelve Jews wrapped in *talleisim*, murmuring

Tefillas Zakah. Within minutes, Reb Avrom heard the mournful, though hushed, tones of a *chazzan* chanting *Kol Nidrei*.

It was a strange night. The men *davened*, then slipped away into the night. The next day, Reb Avrom again joined the silent *minyan*, *davening* with them until *Ne'ilah*, when the worshipers once again slipped away into the shadows. Throughout the night and day, not a word had passed between any of the men. "My silent *Yom Kippur*," Reb Avrom called it.

In 1950, while working in a state-run jewelry store as an appraiser, Reb Avrom, like so many others, was arrested on some nebulous charge. His wife, as strong in her way as he was in his, charged through the doors of the investigating office, demanding his release. As a result of her ceaseless efforts, his sentence was reduced to two years, from the usual ten to fifteen.

At sixty, Reb Avrom retired, spending the rest of his days in study and prayer.

But this man, so devoted throughout his life to G-d and His Torah, felt obligated to protect his children from the possible consequences of his beliefs. They knew they were Jewish; they knew that Pappa had some eccentric behavior that must be tolerated.

And that was all. Of the beauty of Jewish belief, of the *mitzvos* and traditions that fill a Jew's life, they knew nothing. Educated in Soviet schools, they were good atheists, good Communists. Of their father's sacrifice for Torah — nothing remained in their own lives.

Father and Son

Reb Getzl Vilensky was another Moscow Jew unable to transmit his heritage. A Lubavitcher *Chassid*, Reb Getzl would often hold *farbrengens* in his Moscow apartment. Rabbi Essas remembers with a sigh how Reb Getzl's sixth and youngest child, thirty-five years old, would stay in the next room listening to Russian pop music. His five older brothers and sisters, too, showed no interest in what they accepted, regretfully, as their father's eccentricities.

The bridge between generations, that which we call mesorah, had been almost destroyed by the Communists. Could one dare imagine that one day it would ever be rebuilt?

~§ A Shabbos of Mesorah

Even in what seemed to be impenetrable darkness, though, Hashem allowed tiny beacons of light to go forth.

It happened some months after Moscow resident Ilya Essas had committed himself to a life of Torah. The problem he faced now was: What, exactly, did that life consist of? He knew, from his secret studies of Jewish books, that one made something called *"kiddush"* on *Shabbos*. He was, in his own quiet, determined way, on the path to becoming a scholar, and he could have quoted many of the *halachos* of *kiddush* straight from the *Shulchan Aruch*. But he'd never heard it said, had no idea of how one actually recited it!

There is knowledge that cannot come from books, knowledge that comes from living a Torah life, or learning from one who lives such a life. The knowledge of *mesorah*, tradition. This was completely lacking in Essas' life.

The bearer of *mesorah* for Eliyahu Essas, and for the students who would learn from him, was an unlikely prospect: Reb Shalom Yakobson, an elderly, childless widower living a quiet, impoverished life in Riga.

Following the advice of Rabbi Pinchas Teitz of Elizabeth, New Jersey, who had been in contact with Soviet activists for years, Eliyahu Essas traveled to Riga for what would prove to be the most memorable *Shabbos* of his life.

Good things don't come easily. It was a fifteen-hour train journey, a journey of over six hundred miles of Russian darkness. The threat of police with their unpleasant questions was a heavy blanket covering the soul all through the ride.

Essas arrived at Yakobson's home, a three-room apartment in Riga that he shared with a non-Jewish family, at about ten in the morning, exhausted but excited. When the elderly Yakobson met Essas, his face grew radiant. Here was a boy, a mere stripling of twenty-eight, interested in Judaism! What wondrous phenomenon was this?

That evening the two men, one young and one aged, shared a *Shabbos* meal of *challah* (homebaked by Yakobson's sister Clara), herring and hot potatoes, sprats, cake and tea. For Essas, it was the first time he actually saw someone recite *kiddush* and wash before eating bread. Revelation followed revelation. The very first *birkas hamazon*. Reminiscences of pre-war life when Yakobson was one of the leaders of the Agudath Israel movement in Latvia.

The next morning, Reb Shalom walked proudly through the Riga streets, with Eliyahu by his side. Their destination: the Riga Synagogue where Reb Shalom *davened* faithfully each week. Along the way, Reb Shalom would cast warm, tear-filled glances at the young man walking beside him. It was a dream: someone young, walking beside him to prayers. A young man, an avid student — it was almost as though he had found a son to impart his beliefs to!

When Essas arrived in the synagogue, he saw the same picture he'd seen before in Moscow: elderly Jews praying. No children. No grandchildren. The only person who stood with his "son" beside him — even if it were only for one *Shabbos* — was the beaming, proud Reb Shalom Yakobson.

And then, in the next afternoon, a supreme moment. Yakobson, any lingering suspicion of his unusual guest dispelled by the avid interest that Essas showed, reverently approached a small bookshelf that stood unobtrusively in one corner of the room. With trembling hands, he handed Essas a small, dark volume. A *Mishnayos*, a pre-war, Palestine, Eshkol edition. A treasure.

In hushed tones, he recounted the tale of the *sefer*. In 1940, when independent Latvia had been taken over by the Communists, he'd been arrested for his "subversive" activities as a leader in Agudath Israel.

"You have months, perhaps days, to live," the investigator, himself a Russian Jew, warned Yakobson.

"Only G-d can tell how long a man shall live," Yakobson answered defiantly.

The NKVD was nothing if not swift, and when he was arrested Yakobson had time only to grab one precious item: a *Mishnayos*, pre-war, Palestine, Eshkol edition. The *Mishnayos* stayed with him, somehow, all through the years of labor camps and prisons. Once, in Russia, a prison guard found the book during a routine search and prepared to confiscate it.

"You can take the book, but you'll have to shoot me to do it," Yakobson said quietly.

The officer, looking around at all the prisoners, hesitated. He saw the look in Yakobson's eye; he knew he meant what he'd said.

"Keep it today. I'll remember this," the guard finally said, as he stalked off.

The next day Yakobson was transferred away from both that prison and that prison guard.

The *sefer* stayed with him through the brutal winters and merciless summers. It stayed with him from camp to camp — even in the labor camp where he met the first investigator of his case, now a prisoner himself. "I had told him only G-d knew when a man would die," Yakobson told Essas. "I lived; a few months after I met him, the investigator was dead."

CHAPTER 3

The Return

The Midrash tells us that when the Yam Suf split, all the water in the world split as well, in order that there not be a person on the earth who remained unaware of the miracle that had taken place for the Jews. In some ways, the Six Day War, too, was such a worldwide miracle — an event whose impact was global.

Most importantly, perhaps, the liberation of Jerusalem and other parts of Eretz Yisrael in six remarkable days was Hashem's means of opening up vital channels between Him and His people: once again, Jews were praying at the Kotel, at Kever Rochel, and at Ma'aras Hamachpelah. In America, the miracle paved the way towards new feelings of Jewish consciousness and pride that were vital in the creation of what would one day be called the "ba'al teshuvah movement."

In the Soviet Union, a curtain built of reinforced steel could not keep out the reverberations of the event. The incredible victory of a Jewish army galvanized Soviet Jewry. Suddenly, one's Jewish heritage was not an unwanted burden, an embarrassment, an obstacle on the way to one's goal. Zionist feeling ran high; curiosity about this land, this people — my people — was a powerful impetus to learning more about the Jewish heritage. By 1968, a small circle of Soviet Jews was meeting regularly to talk about the realities of emigration, and soon the first requests for visas went out.

The crusade began with the Hebrew language. It was the language of creation; the language of Torah; the language of

Jewish scholarship for millennia. Changed into modern "Ivrit," it became the language of hope to a generation of Zionists.

For the Soviet Jew, the Hebrew language was the first means of getting to know a forbidden history.

⋙ In Hebrew School

Viktor was a successful computer scientist, a Moscow-born Jew in his late twenties. Until the Six Day War, he'd shown little interest in the fact that the fifth line on his internal passport marked his nationality as Jewish. But in the war's aftermath, spurred on by his wife, he decided to learn more about the possibility of emigration. Still, he hesitated to make the final commitment, filing for an exit visa, because he feared the repercussions. Everyone knew that a man who filed for an exit visa was viewed as a traitor. He lost his job, his friends shunned him; he became a pariah.

Finally, in the early 1970s, he found the courage to make the commitment. He went the usual route, filing for a visa with the local OVIR office in Moscow, being called to answer for his temerity before a meeting of about one hundred fellow employees, many of whom openly accused him of betraying his country. He lost his job, and now stood in danger of arrest for being a "parasite." And, finally, he received his answer: He had worked for two years in a vital industry, and his emigration would endanger the Soviet Union. Viktor was now a full-fledged refusenik.

He became a regular at the weekly demonstrations on Archipov Street. Moscow's synagogue was located on the small street, named for a Russian painter. But it was not for services that the forty or fifty refuseniks — most of whom knew little of their own religion — gathered every Saturday afternoon. They drew together to give each other moral support and practical help in dealing with a relentlessly hostile bureaucracy.

Eventually, his colleagues' suspicion of him — and, with KGB infiltration always a problem, they were suspicious of almost everyone — finally relaxed, and Viktor was ready for the next step: Hebrew lessons.

In 1972, Viktor was part of the "second generation" of refuseniks. The "first generation," those whose Jewish consciousness had awakened with the Six Day War, were by now the leaders of the movement. Viktor turned to one of these "elders," Pavel Abramovich, who was unofficially in charge of the Hebrew lessons, for help.

Abramovich sent him to Alyosha Levin, another first-generation teacher. It was a dark Tuesday night. Viktor, his heart thumping, his face an emotionless mask, made his way through the center of Moscow. Past the embassies, past the building which had been Leo Tolstoi's home. Here, in the heart of the Soviet capital, was the pre-Revolutionary home of an aristocratic and noble family, now converted to a block of flats.

Here, Alyosha Levin clandestinely ran his "Hebrew school."

There was good reason for the secrecy. Though teaching Hebrew was not officially illegal, one could get into dire trouble for illegal gatherings or Zionist, bourgeois activity. Several Hebrew teachers eventually were arrested for such "crimes": Yuli Edelstein, Alexander Cholmiansky of Moscow, and Moshe Abramov, who was exiled to three years in faraway Samarkand. The record holder was Iosef Begun who was sentenced to three years for teaching Hebrew. After his exile in a tiny Siberian hamlet was over, Begun returned, began to teach Hebrew again, and was sent to a labor camp. For his third arrest, Begun spent seven years in still another *gulag*.

The teaching of Hebrew was something of a family tradition in the Levin home. Levin's wife's grandfather, Felix Shapiro, had, years before and against all odds, brought about the publication of a Hebrew-Russian dictionary.

Shapiro had clandestinely worked for years on the project, scrupulously maintaining his entries on small index cards. In the early 1960s he and a professor of Semitic languages in the army's Military Academy (Hebrew, after all, would be useful for diplomats and spies!) convinced the authorities that because the Soviet Union had diplomatic relations with Israel, and because the Soviet Union was a cultured, modern country, they should come out with a Hebrew-Russian dictionary.

The authorities fell for it. In 1963, the officially sanctioned Hebrew-Russian dictionary came out. Although by now, the 1970s, it was almost impossible to get hold of except in academic or military circles, the dictionary still had its impact on Soviet Jewish life, for it was more than just a book — it gave legitimacy to the concept of the Hebrew language.

Shapiro's grandson-in-law solemnly handed out to the six or seven students their first textbook — a photographed copy of an Israeli text, "Elef Milim — One Thousand Words."

Obtaining texts and finding people who knew enough of the language to teach it was a constant problem. In one of those ironies which are so frequent in the history of Soviet Jewry, it was a violently anti-religious and anti-Israeli Russian *goy* who actually helped teach the first generation.

Avigdor Levitt was born to a Russian mother and a Jewish father. After World War II, Levitt's parents, both left-wing Socialists, and their young son, Avigdor, emigrated to Israel, where Levitt's father became a prominent member of the Socialist party, Mapam.

The Levitts were divorced when Avigdor was sixteen, and the former Mrs. Levitt, together with her son, traveled back to her native land. Here, Levitt grew to adulthood. He was a strange man, who spoke out vocally against the current politics of Israel and Judaism, and yet always kept up contact with Israelis and Soviet refuseniks. Some thought he was a KGB spy; others felt he was a mere eccentric. But he had one extraordinarily important quality: He spoke Hebrew like a native. And for some reason, he was willing to teach others. Levitt became the unlikely scholar-in-residence, one of the founding fathers of the Hebrew teaching.

But that was in the past; now, almost three years later, the second generation was learning: The *"mesorah"* of the Hebrew language was being passed on.

Viktor clutched the sheaf of papers in his hands, then placed them reverently beneath his jacket. Following his teacher's instructions, he took a pen and a small notebook and wrote carefully, in the Cyrillic alphabet, two strange, strange-sounding words: *Ani Yehudi.*

Ani Yehudi. They would meet for two or three hours each week, and would learn about fifty words each lesson. They would begin studying phonetically; by the third lesson they would be speaking to each other; by the fourth they would be writing Hebrew. But no word, no phrase or sentence or book, would have the impact of those words on men like Viktor. *Ani Yehudi.* I am a Jew.

> Sometimes a *"bas kol"* comes from above to give a Jew
> Heavenly messages; other times, radio waves will suffice.

✺ Channel to Freedom

Vlad Borisovich, a Leningrad mathematician, sat hunched over his small shortwave radio. The windows in his small apartment were all closed, despite the summer's heat: Too dangerous to allow the neighbors to hear the forbidden sounds. From the receiver Vlad could make out unnerving static, the screech of strange whistling sounds, and something very precious: the voice of an Israeli broadcaster, speaking of foreign, exotic, and dangerous ideas such as Zionism, the Hebrew language, and a city called Jerusalem.

Vlad, born and bred in the atheistic "worker's paradise," had never heard of the word "*hashgachah pratis*." Yet, in the year 1970, the young professor — and many more like him who would later become Zionists, refuseniks, and, sometimes, Torah-observant Jews — was undoubtedly the beneficiary of a precious Heavenly gift.

For years, foreign governments had sent their illegal broadcasts into Soviet airwaves. There was Radio Free Europe, Voice of America, The BBC Foreign Service, and Israel Radio's Foreign Service, bringing news from the Jewish state.

In 1968, when they invaded Czechoslovakia, the Soviet military began jamming all foreign broadcasts, in order to keep from its citizenry the outraged voice of the rest of the world. Radio Free Europe. Voice of America. The B.B.C. Foreign Service. Only one broadcaster was exempt: Israeli Radio, which had not paid much attention to the Soviet action.

Thus, from 1968 to 1972, when the military finally included Israel Radio in its jamming, the only voice of the outside world available to people like Vlad was a Jewish voice. The time was ripe for a revival of Jewish consciousness — and Hashem supplied the broadcasts.

Ask any member of the KGB and they'll tell you this rule: Books are dangerous objects.

ঙ The Encyclopedia

The years was 1972. Ilya, a Moscow mathematician, was desperately searching for knowledge of things Jewish. He was learning Hebrew clandestinely once a week, but it was not enough. What he really needed, what he longed for with a desire that was almost a physical ache, were books: crisp pages and clear print to cut through the lies and the propaganda and the illusions that had shaped his life until now. But how to get them, in this worker's paradise, where books were forbidden?

Ilya began frequenting Moscow bookstores, searching through stacks of old, musty volumes, hoping desperately that something would turn up.

And one day, it did.

It was a sixteen-volume Jewish encyclopedia. In one of the quirks of the legal system that refuseniks soon learned to recognize and profit from, it could not be stamped as counterrevolutionary — because it had been published years before the revolution, in the early 1900s. It had been sold to the bookstore by a Jew emigrating to Israel who was forced to leave it behind.

Ilya hesitantly opened the first volume and reverently thumbed through the entries. Vistas opened before his eyes, which had unaccountably grown misty. There were paragraphs about Moses, about Palestine, about the Talmud. Entries on blood libels and Spinoza and the population of Jewish communities. A new world!

Very rarely in a man's life can he put a price on something priceless. Here, in this dusty bookstore, a treasure, a people, a heritage were available to Ilya for one hundred and seventy rubles — a month's salary.

Ilya tore himself away from the hypnotizing volume, raced outside, and hailed a cab. At home, he frantically searched through pockets, wallets, emergency hiding places. He went to a neighbor, a trusted friend, and borrowed what he could. Finally he had it — one hundred and seventy rubles.

One hundred seventy rubles would buy him a new winter coat — his old one was worn and patched and barely kept out the frigid Moscow wind. It would buy new shoes for the entire family. It would pay the food bills, more than cover the rent.

Ilya raced back to the bookstore. Soon, the treasure was his.

Today, Ilya — Eliyahu Essas — sits in a living room surrounded by *sefarim*. His journey to Jerusalem, and his spiritual journey to Torah observance, he is convinced, both began, not with the pages of an outdated secular Jewish encyclopedia — but with the *mesiras nefesh* that allowed him to purchase it.

For many Soviet *ba'alei teshuvah*, the awakening of Zionist consciousness was the first step towards a return to Torah observance. For others, it was a much more physical object that began their journey of discovery: matzah.

At the same time that they sought to eradicate Torah observance, the Communists kept the facade of tolerance, the pretense that they were, indeed, a multi-national state in which every ethnic group has a part. Even during the dark Stalin years, matzah and matzah crackers were usually made available by the authorities. After all, what

*harm could the dry, unpalatable stuff do to Bolshevik
ideology?*

*How little they knew of Jewish history, and of the taste of
the Pesach afikoman that lasted so long — a lifetime, perhaps
—in the mouths of the Jewish people!*

⊷§ Matzah Marranos

From Stalin's days and right on through Gorbachev's era of *glasnost*,
there were two inescapable facts of Jewish life: the word *Yevrei* printed
on the fifth line of the passport, and the *matzah* that one ate on *Pesach*.
On thousands of tables in thousands of overcrowded apartments, there
might be no *seder*, no *Haggadah*, no four cups of wine — but *matzah*
there would be, *matzah* and, perhaps, a taste of bitterness in the mouth.

One elderly *"babushka"* now living in Far Rockaway still remembers
those *matzahs*. Her husband would travel to Kuibyshev, to one of the
sixty or seventy official Soviet synagogues sanctioned by the government. There, a small house built adjacent to it, a ramshackle affair,
suddenly became the focus of a thousand eyes. It was here, under
conditions more primitive than those that had prevailed a century earlier,
that the "official" state *matzah* was prepared. It was here that, during
those perennial wheat shortages that plague the Soviet Union, Jews
would somehow obtain their own flour for baking.

For this woman's husband, obtaining those dry, burnt *matzahs* took
twenty-four solid hours of waiting, and another twenty-four hours of
travel: forty-eight hours stolen from a relentless Communist master,
forty-eight hours to proclaim, "I am a Jew."

With the night-long vigils usually necessary for the official *matzah*,
and the vagaries of a surly bureaucracy that could, and sometimes did,
halt the sale, many Jews would not, or could not, obtain the synagogue
matzah. For them, the path was more perilous still. Each year, brave souls
would build tiny ovens in outlying areas and bake their own *matzah*.
The risks were considerable: Illegal financial activities, two to seven
years' imprisonment. Unsanitary conditions, one to three years imprisonment. Illegal gathering for anti-Soviet activity, up to seven years'
imprisonment.

Some Jews, afraid to bring the watchful eye of the NKVD on them,
would become *"Matzah Marranos,"* sending an elderly grandparent to
patiently wait on line for the state *matzahs*. But on the night different
from all other nights, they, too, would eat of it.

✑ From Bondage to Freedom

Like many Soviet *ba'alei teshuvah*, Ilya Essas clearly recalls his first religious experience at the *seder* table:

In spring of 1972, four months after he'd begun Hebrew lessons, his teacher, Alyosha Levin, brought a pre-Revolutionary book that he'd never seen: a *Haggadah*. His "rebbe" had himself made only one *seder* in his life, the year before. Now he would teach others how to do it.

The intent young people studied for three or four lessons. They read the *Hagaddah* and studied the traditions. *Marror* was no problem: There is plenty of bitterness in Russia. They ate it undiluted; several actually lost their breath from its strength. For *charoses*, there would be the brick-like substance that Telshe Yeshivah had somehow smuggled in: in America, an interesting fund-raising ploy; in the Soviet Union, a tiny link to an eternal tradition.

Before the actual night, they held a rehearsal. How thrilled everyone was to do everything with his own hands!

Then came the big night. Ilya Essas invited three or four friends. He read the *Haggadah* in Hebrew and then tried to explain it. For three hours they sat in his tiny Moscow apartment, speaking in an unfamiliar tongue, doing unfamiliar rites.

The next day, the second day of *Yom Tov* for the Jews living outside of Israel, seven Hebrew teachers and about twenty of their "star" pupils gathered together for a "high-quality" *seder*.

Like the *seder* itself, the night was a mixture of slavery and freedom. The participants were, at the same time, extraordinarily proud and yet terribly afraid of the police. Some were already active refuseniks, particularly vulnerable to KGB harassment. They could all be charged with an illegal gathering, with anti-Soviet and Zionist propaganda: three to seven years.

During the *seder* they prepared for the knock at the door. In that dangerous event, every *Hagaddah* would be removed; this would be merely a social gathering of friends.

The evening passed, a mixture of tension and delight. And then came the moment of supreme danger, supreme faith. One man stood up and proudly opened the door. Rabbi Essas still remembers that moment: "When we opened the door for Eliyahu the Prophet, we all felt the protection of Hashem. Though none of us was observant, none of us was religious, we all felt it. We opened the door, unafraid, and looked at one another."

❧ One Seder Leads to Another

The next year Essas, already a Hebrew teacher himself, a "veteran" of Judaism after sixteen months of study, invited his pupils to his home for a *seder*. This was the first of many *sedarim* that he was to make for others. In the future, in the 1970s and 1980s, Rabbi Essas would urge all his young, unmarried *talmidim* to lead *sedarim* for Jews who had no knowledge, who had nothing but a strong desire to celebrate the holiday. He himself would not commit himself until the very day before *Yom Tov*, knowing that among the incessant phone calls with "*sh'eilos*" about the holiday would come a plea for his presence. Rabbi Essas would spend the first *seder* at home, while traveling like his forefathers in Egypt, into a spiritual desert for the second.

It wasn't easy. In April of 1983, for example, Moscow was a cold, cold place. He walked through the frigid air, the wind whipping his unprotected ears. He walked up twelve harsh, dimly lit flights of stone steps, into a small apartment, to face a crowd of almost forty people, all of them staring at him. Their faces showed a kaleidoscope of different emotions. Some were nervous, some were expectant; a few, usually dragged there by friends or spouses, were openly hostile. No one smiled. The tension was as palpable as the heat in the overcrowded room, a heat so thick that despite the frigid wind outside, it brought a coating of steam to the windows.

Rabbi Essas was expected to lead this group for close to five hours, inspire them and make them forget the possibility of a KGB knock. He was to transport them from Moscow to Egypt. The place was so crowded that when it was time to lean to the left, the entire group had to do it all together around a table in a strange show of unity under tension.

Finally, in the darkness, he returned to his wife and children, who had made their *seder* by themselves: another walk through the quiet, freezing streets. And then, on *Chol HaMoed*, he reaped his reward. The telephone rang constantly with questions about the festival, about the *seder*, and about the Torah. And, particularly, questions on what those who attended could do next to learn more.

From that 1983 *seder* on the twelfth floor, thirty-three participants ultimately made the commitment to a Torah life. And they, too, began to teach, and began to lead *sedarim* for strangers.

Such was the path traveled by many Soviet Jews, a path from bondage to freedom.

One Jew whose return began with Pesach was Sasha, last seen in this narrative standing, astounded, blood dripping from his jaw, listening to a bully taunt him with the strange word, "Zhid." Now, some ten years later, we follow Sasha and hundreds of others to Moscow's matzah bakery.

✒ Sasha's Tale . . . The Return

The story begins, as did so many others, with *matzahs*. Sasha knew that every year, when the snowdrops were in bloom and the fierce Russian winds grew a little milder, his father would bring home some dry, bland stuff called *matzah*. Often, they ate it together with the eggs that Sasha's mother brought home, gifts from her colleagues. The eggs were painted lovely pastel colors, in honor of her colleagues' holiday — Easter. Other times, the *matzah* was eaten with slices of bacon. All Sasha knew about the stuff was that it was somehow connected with springtime and with the fact that he was *Yevrei*, and that it came from a mysterious place known as the *synagoga*.

At fifteen, on a strange impulse, he asked his father if he could go to *synagoga* to pick up the *matzah*. His father, not realizing where the short trip would ultimately lead his son, readily agreed.

What began as a lighthearted adventure ended as a revelation. For the first time Sasha saw Jews, about five hundred of them, gathered together as Jews. He saw letters of a language that somehow felt familiar, though he'd never seen it before: Hebrew. He learned that *Pesach* was a festival of the Jews and that Easter eggs had no connection with *matzah*.

Enormously excited by his discovery, and curious as well, he determined to find out more. His parents begged him not to endanger himself by joining the Jews who traditionally met near the synagogue on festivals. The gathering was quasi-legal; that is, though the City of Moscow allowed the street to be closed and sent police for crowd control, the KGB attended, taking photos of those present, while every university had a representative looking to see which of its students was in attendance — expelling the luckless ones who were recognized.

That *Pesach*, 20,000 Jews jammed tiny Archipov Street to celebrate their holiday by dancing and singing Israeli and Russian-Jewish folk songs. A *seder* was still unknown to most of them, among them one young man studying in a prestigious school for music: Sasha.

Sasha stood in a corner of the synagogue's *ezras nashim*. His parents, resigned to the fact that their headstrong teenager would be present, had suggested that he'd be less conspicuous there. The scene below made an enormous impression on him. Here were thousands of Jews dancing, singing, celebrating joyously. No one was drunk, no one was fighting and shoving. Throwing caution to the winds, Sasha joined the dancing circles. As he whirled round and round he made a vow. He would join these people, his people. Born a Jew, he would now be a Jew. Whatever that meant. And whatever the consequences.

Once again, a Jew celebrated liberation — national and personal — on the holiday of *Pesach*.

> *The Hebrew lessons and Jewish culture that for some refuseniks represented the culmination of years of hope that they would be allowed to leave the Soviet Union for Israel, and the dry matzahs that were for many the entirety of Jewish observance, were, for a small minority, only a beginning. It was important to know that you are a Jew. But what, exactly, is a Jew? For that, one had to search further than a dictionary or a vocabulary list or an encyclopedia, or even a circle of young people dancing and singing in front of a synagogue.*
>
> *For that, one needed Torah.*

❧ The Unlikely Rebbe

With the chain of *mesorah* all but destroyed, Hashem chose some unusual men to hand down Torah learning. But none was more unusual than the man who introduced Eliyahu Essas to his first words of Torah — Aryeh Leib ben Tzvi Hirsch, Lev Grigoriyovich Gurevich.

More than half a decade earlier, Lev Gurevich had been a student in Volozhin; now, an elderly man in Moscow, he was a self-proclaimed "religious atheist." He had been a Socialist, he had been a Zionist. In the early 1960s, he and his brother, Michael, had acted as unofficial liaisons between the Israeli embassy and the Jewish community in Moscow. The two of them, code-named "The Brothers," had given out Hebrew texts and pictures of *Magen Davids* to incipient refuseniks.

Iosef Begun sent Ilya Essas to this Lev Gurevich, explaining that he was interested in young people who were learning Hebrew.

They met in Gurevich's small Moscow apartment, the young man thirsting for knowledge, the old man eager to teach.

"What would you like to learn?" Lev Gurevich asked.

Eliyahu Essas shrugged. He had learned Hebrew for eight months now, but he hardly knew enough of Judaism to even know what he didn't know.

Lev Gurevich turned to his bookshelf and pulled off an old book. Its pages were yellowed, its binding dusty. The edges of the paper were brown and cracking.

He opened the *sefer* and held it out before Eliyahu. *Chazon Yeshayahu ben Amotz* — The vision of Yeshayahu, son of Amotz.

A new world had opened for Eliyahu Essas.

Lev Gurevich, as taken with his new pupil as Essas was with his learning, looked for every opportunity to teach him more. And what better place to study than in a yeshivah?

ᴈ The Yeshivah Bachur

When Henry Kissinger arrived in 1972, the Soviet authorities decided to reopen the *yeshivah* they had founded in Khrushchev's time and later closed. Lev Gurevich was called upon to take the position of Chief Lecturer. After all, he had learned something in his youth, he was fluent in Hebrew, and he attended synagogue regularly. Besides, Chief Rabbi Fishman, who could barely read a sentence in the holy tongue, was certainly not equipped for the job.

Gurevich was soon adjuring his new and rapt pupil, Ilya Essas, to join the *yeshivah*. The authorities, Gurevich knew, desperately needed students to lend legitimacy to their claim that religious freedom was flourishing in the Soviet Union. But they would not accept refuseniks, known Zionist sympathizers, or any activists who might endanger the sleepy atmosphere of Jewish religious life in the Union.

Essas, who was planning on applying for an exit visa but who had not yet taken that fateful step, was a perfect candidate.

Nine o'clock in the morning. Ilya Essas walked nervously into the "yeshivah," wondering how he would do among the learned scholars, the elite of Soviet *talmidei chachamim*.

No one was there.

By ten, the *yeshivah* students had begun to arrive. There was an obviously retarded twenty-five-year-old man, brought to sit in the room by his elderly father. A fifty-five-year-old soldier who had lost both arms in battle, who had come to spend his days among Jews, but who couldn't read *aleph-beis*. Two young men from rural areas who hardly knew a word of Hebrew used this opportunity to come to the big city.

By eleven o'clock, when all the *yeshivah* boys had drifted in, Essas saw that there was no place for him among the untutored young men and the hoodlums who frequented the "*yeshivah*." He sat at his table hopelessly wondering what he was doing there.

That was when Lev Gurevich brought him the *sefer*. A *Chumash*. The very first he had ever seen.

Soon Eliyahu Essas was in a new world. A world of learning, where nothing else mattered.

Essas had been learning *Chumash* for less than three months when his "*rebbe*" was hospitalized with a heart attack. Gurevich asked his star pupil, Ilya, to take over a *shiur* in *parashas hashavua* that he gave to five elderly men each week. Now the young mathematician began to really understand the vastness of meaning within the words of the Torah. He would spend each week delving into the text, drinking in the words of Ramban, Seforno, the *Kli Yakar* . . . less than two years after he had had his first Hebrew lesson.

It was the beginning of August, when summer lends its all-too-short warmth to the Moscow air, the poplars bloom and the scent of lilac fills the air. The young teacher would nervously give his class each Wednesday, terrified that his pupils, who had all attended *cheder* many decades before, would catch on to the limited extent of his knowledge.

A lifetime of living with anti-Semitism; years of Zionist hopes and aspirations; a year of "Hebrew school"; a few months of familiarity with the *Tanach*; a few weeks of study of *Shulchan Aruch* — and the words of Torah. He was studying the weekly *sedrah*, reading its words for the first time. "*Va'eschanan* — I pleaded before Hashem. . . Let me pass over and see the good land. . . And those of you who have cleaved to Hashem, you are alive today. . . You shall heed and you shall do, for it is your wisdom and your understanding. . . Lest you forget. . . the day that you stood before Hashem, your L-rd on Chorev. . ."

With these words, says Rabbi Essas, all of his experiences came together. Through the words of *Parashas Va'eschanan*, and the two *parshios* that followed, *Ekev* and *Re'ei*, studied and then taught so painstakingly by a man trying hard to catch up on decades of ignorance, Ilya Essas, refusenik, Zionist, and Soviet Jew, had his own personal *matan Torah*. He had become, with only the help of a few unlikely mentors, an observant Jew.

The next task was to pass his revelation on to others waiting to learn.

CHAPTER 4

Spreading a Forbidden Word

In 1977, five years after he'd opened his first sefer, Eliyahu Essas had achieved one of his life's goals: He was learning Gemara with Rishonim and Acharonim. Now his thoughts turned to the future. There were some indications that, at last, he might soon be allowed to emigrate. Yet, could he leave without having passed on to others what knowledge he'd gained?

Absurd as it might sound in Soviet Russia, it was time to begin teaching Torah.

⋅§ The First Class

Inside the courtroom, refusenik Iosef Begun was being tried for his seditious activities. The trial was to commence at nine in the morning, and a group of refuseniks who had gathered together in front of the court by eight o'clock in an attempt to attend the proceedings was not allowed entry. Legally scrupulous, as always, the KGB had simply packed the court hours before with its own employees, so that it could honestly refuse admittance to the troublemakers on the grounds that there was no room for them inside.

Undaunted, the refuseniks milled around outside, hoping their presence would strengthen and comfort their incarcerated colleague. Among them was Eliyahu Essas.

While waiting in front of the courtroom, Essas finally nerved himself to carry out his long-awaited plan. He approached several of the refuseniks who had shown interest in religious observance with his daring suggestion: Let them meet once a week to learn Torah.

Lag B'Omer, Moscow, 1975. The "refuseniks' rabbi," Eliyahu Essas (standing at left), gives a lecture on Rabbi Akiva and his disciples at a picnic that included virtually all of Moscow's active refuseniks. Not pictured are the tens of KGB agents who stood behind the birch trees, taking pictures and notes.

It was, recalls Rabbi Essas, a plan that needed a good dose of Jewish *chutzpah*. First, the participants would be risking KGB interference, and possibly jail sentences. And second, who was he, who had never been properly taught, to teach others?

Still, there was no choice, and so he took the first difficult step — recruiting students.

About three weeks later, on the Thursday after *Shavuos*, a group of Soviet men (classes for women would have to wait for another two years) began their own belated acceptance of Torah. They met in an apartment belonging to their young colleague, Semion Amdursky, whose parents had emigrated to Israel several years before, leaving him a large (that is, two-bedroom) apartment for himself.

They sat around a rectangular table, Essas at its head. There were about sixteen of them, seventeen-year-old Avigdor Eskin the youngest, and Essas, 31, the oldest of the group.

The *"rebbe"* opened with an announcement. "As we learn, I welcome your questions on the topic of discussion. Once we've completed our lecture, I welcome your questions on any topic at all. There is just one question that I am asking you not to ask me for the next two months: Is there a G-d?

"Right now, you are not equipped with the ideas or the terms to discuss this question with me. For the next two months, assume that there is an Almighty guiding us. After two months of learning Torah, feel free to ask."

Essas saw it was a good way to open the class, so good that he used it every time he commenced a new set of classes.

And in the years that he taught in the atheistic Communist "paradise," not one student saw the need to ask him if G-d exists. Not after two months of Torah learning.

As if to make up for the lost years of the Communist regime, Hashem somehow telescoped time for the returnees, allowing them to accomplish in months what it would take their freer counterparts years.

৸ Michael in Class

Michael, a holder of a Ph.D. and a researcher in the Central Moscow Library, glanced cautiously at the street sign and walked slowly down the tree-lined Moscow street, looking for number 10. When he finally reached his destination, he took a hasty look at the innocuous apartment house, so like all the others, glanced nervously over his shoulder, and walked quickly on. He reached the end of the block, paused, turned around and returned to number 10.

He knocked at a door on the third floor. Why, he wondered as he waited for a reply, was he risking his career, and who knew what else, for this mad adventure?

The door opened just a little. He muttered his name, the door opened wider, and he stepped in.

Seven men sat around the table in the modestly furnished living room. A bearded man wearing — was that a skullcap? — smiled a welcome and motioned him to sit down.

Someone handed Michael an old Hebrew book. Michael, though not yet a refusenik, had become interested in his Jewish heritage some months ago, and had begun Hebrew lessons about six weeks before. It was actually at the Hebrew class that he'd heard the startling news that in Moscow men were gathering together to study from Jewish holy books. Almost on a whim, Michael, who knew nothing at all of Jewish observance, decided to attend.

And now here he was. He glanced down at the book, at the *aleph-beis* that he'd so painstakingly studied, then turned his attention to the Rabbi's words.

The Torah (strange word!) was divided into portions read each week, the teacher, Rabbi Essas, explained. And because each and every word was fraught with significance and meaning, there was no need to begin at the beginning. Instead, he would teach the actual *parashah* of that week.

What Rabbi Essas then proceeded to do, at least for Michael, was to weave an extraordinary tapestry, to bring together ancient words and commentaries with the day-to-day existence of a Muscovite Jew. Ethics and morality and practical advice: Here, indeed, was a treasure trove, a magical assembling of wisdom!

All too soon, it was over. The host walked out from the kitchen with a samovar filled with steaming tea. Soon, the table was covered with plates of cake and pungent sardines.

Michael, though, was far too excited to do justice to the repast. Raptly, he listened to the words of the Rabbi. In the second part of his class,

Rabbi Essas (standing at left) translates a lecture by Lord Immanuel Jakobovits, Chief Rabbi, British Emprie, 1975. The topic was the Torah view on ethical problems in medicine.

Rabbi Essas found it worthwhile to take a topic of practical Judaism and introduce his students to it informally. Tonight the subject was *tefillin*, and Michael watched, fascinated, as Rabbi Essas showed them an actual pair and demonstrated its use.

Michael was hooked. The next week, and the week after, he was the first to arrive, the last to leave. A researcher during his working hours, his analytical mind gloried in the clear-cut wisdom that he saw in Torah; a poet in his spare time, his heart soared with its beauty.

Rabbi Essas was in a hurry: Who knew when he would be granted his precious exit visa and the freedom to emigrate? Teachers had to be groomed, and groomed quickly. Within two months Michael and three other select students were introduced to two extraordinary concepts: *chavrusa* learning, and the Talmud.

Six months after Michael had nervously looked for that strange apartment, he was studying *Gemara*, keeping the *mitzvos* — and teaching his own group of fledgling students.

With all the solemnity of classes that touched upon eternal questions, there were moments of humor too.

◆§ The Ride Home

The lecture had ended. The thirteen participants prepared to go home. As always, they left one or two at a time; it would not do to have a large group seen leaving from one apartment. It might be dangerous for the apartment's owner.

About half a dozen met, as always, at a bus stop about one hundred meters down the street. Together, they rode to the subway station, where they boarded a train. It was part of a brand new line, a short one that connected up with one of Moscow's major lines.

They made an interesting group, these six young men. The curious onlooker might notice that all of them had beards, wore caps and carried books. Luckily, this onlooker could not read the strange script on each of the books' binding — for it was a *Kehati Mishnayos* that these men, who had already committed themselves to a Torah life, were carrying.

The train pulled into the last stop. Here, at last, was the moment these intense young men had been waiting for.

Their eyes gleamed, their lips began to quiver. The taped message on the public address station began its recorded litany. "Marxist Station. Last stop. Marxist Station. This is the end. Last stop."

Unmindful of the stares, the men broke into laughter. The others on the train, their consciousness deadened by a lifetime of indoctrination, stared. What was so funny?

Marxist Station. Last Stop. This is the end.

The irony was delicious, a marvelous end to a fulfilling night of learning.

The young people learned; the network spread. Soon, there were classes in apartments throughout Moscow. Every story was different, but all paths led to Torah.

⋑ A Family Affair

The KGB was not the only group that kept a watchful eye on the surge of religious interest that had begun to be felt among Moscow's Jews. This yearning for spiritual meaning and content intrigued a swarthy, bearded Muscovite, an imposing man by the name of Shedrovitsky, as well.

Shedrovitsky was a captivating speaker — and an apostate Jew. He would frequent the synagogue, preaching a message of hope, love and spirituality. What he neglected to mention was that he was peddling Christianity as well.

"Judaism is the foundation, the first floor of a great religious edifice," he would proclaim to rapt audiences of young people. Like his fellow missionaries, he would mock "rabbinical Judaism," and give stirring accounts of the life of the founder of the second stage of the "true" religion, a Jew himself, born in the Holy Land, who had a different vision for the world.

Missionaries, particularly members of the "Jews for J...." sect, have two strong allies: the Jewish *neshamah*'s yearning for spirituality, and ignorance of Jewish tradition and history. In Moscow, the yearning and the ignorance were both strong, and Shedrovitsky began to make inroads, forming a loyal cadre of young people who believed his propaganda and half-truths.

Among these followers were two teenagers: Michael and Piotr. They would attend Shedrovitsky's lectures and dutifully spout the "theology" that seemed to fill a void in their lives.

In their enthusiasm, they tried to share their exciting knowledge with others. When Michael's future in-laws, Vlad and Yana, heard details of this Shedrovitsky, they were horrified. Like all Muscovites, they didn't know much about their Jewish heritage, but they did know one thing — a Jew was not a Christian. Never was, and never could be.

Vlad was acquainted with the "refusenik rabbi" who hung around the Moscow Synagogue, teaching Jewish topics. "Save my children," he pleaded with Rabbi Essas. Essas spoke to the two young people, and invited them to join him at a lecture. A bit hesitantly, they agreed.

The Jewish soul is a wonderful thing, the swiftly moving vehicle that brings the Jew back to his Creator. Like any vehicle, it must have a source of power, something to fuel the spark within. And then, when given the proper supply of energy, it roars off into unstoppable motion.

Shedrovitsky's lectures had inspired, excited, and provoked two searching young people into thought. But this! This was Torah! This was what they had been looking for — without ever knowing it. This was the stuff that would fuel their delicately engineered Jewish *neshamahs* into life! In the radiance of this new-found Torah, Shedrovitsky's honeyed words paled into insignificant nothingness.

Within two years, Michael and Piotr had become teachers in Rabbi Essas' growing network.

Once, Vlad and Yana's concern for them had led them from darkness to light. Now it was time for them to repay the debt.

Piotr earnestly explained the problem to Rabbi Essas. Vlad was a physicist, a highly educated, thoughtful person. He acknowledged his Jewish roots — he hadn't been fooled by Shedrovitsky! — but he had no real interest in *mitzvah* observance and Torah learning. Piotr and the others had tried hard to convince him and his wife, using all the rational arguments they could muster, but there had been little progress.

Rabbi Essas thought for a moment, then smiled. "Sometimes, one must forget intellect," he counseled his eager lieutenant. He handed Piotr a pair of *tefillin*. "Give Vlad these," he said.

A bit shamefacedly, somewhat reluctantly, Piotr followed his *rebbe's* advice. And then he sat back and watched, astonished, as a delighted Vlad began to don the *tefillin* daily. An inspired Vlad began to observe *mitzvah* after *mitzvah*, as still another Jew found his place in the world of Torah.

The debt had been repaid. The circle was closed.

To learn the forbidden, at the peril of one's freedom. To go against societal pressures, governmental strictures, and the values inculcated from youth onwards. To rebel. It takes a good dose of courage, a heedlessness of the future: all traits of youth.

So what did this bunch of middle-aged professionals really want?

ᴥ§ *Adult Education*

There are no newsletters in underground cells (at least none propagated publicly!); no posters, no ads, no radio jingles. And yet, somehow, inevitably, word of underground activities gets about, though no one quite knows how.

So Rabbi Essas was not quite shocked when, in 1983, a middle-aged man who introduced himself as Yuli Chassin approached him with a question about his classes. He was not shocked — but he was suspicious.

"We have a group of people who've been doing some studying of Jewish topics," Chassin told him quietly. "Can you help us?"

Not for the first time, Essas faced a dilemma caused by the necessity to expand a secret network. Was this an honest cry for help — or a KGB ploy leading to imprisonment? An opportunity, or a trap? Could he afford to answer the request? Could he afford not to?

What made it particularly strange, and particularly intriguing, was the fact that Chassin was not a young, hot-headed militant, not a well-known refusenik or high-profile dissident. Chassin was an established, middle-aged computer scientist, with a family and a lot to lose.

Rather than endanger one of his lieutenants, Rabbi Essas decided to go himself. That Sunday afternoon, he walked to the address he'd been given. The apartment belonged to an engineer, Ilya Steingart, and his wife Bella, a doctor, both of them, like Chassin, in their productive middle years.

What Essas found waiting in that apartment captivated and enchanted him. About twenty solid citizens, all professionals and all well established, had been meeting together clandestinely every Sunday afternoon. Not knowing what they were looking for, not knowing how to feed their growing hunger, they would simply read out of Jewish history books, searching for roots, for meaning, for answers. It was like finding an unlooked-for oasis within a barren desert; an oasis that

R' Essas, Eliyahu Steingart, Dr. Yisrael Singer of the World Jewish Congress, smiling in Jerusalem.

needed cultivation, certainly, but one which already held the seeds of its own rejuvenation.

The *"shidduch"* between the young teacher and his mature students was an immediate and astonishing success. Here were no interesting vignettes of a history that had been denied them. This was the real stuff: Torah, G-d's word to His people. A way of thought, a way of life.

Chassin and his friends were enormously excited by their discovery. Most of the members of that class began attending other classes, and over time many became observant. Their hosts on that first fateful day, Ilya and Bella Steingart, became important and devoted members of Essas' team. Bella served as unofficial doctor of the network's summer camp, and as for Steingart, his "can-do" engineering flair became a vital component of camp life, whether it was getting a faulty electrical circuit to work or lining up an efficient method of bartering kosher food.

Person by person, class by class — a network was spreading. Or, in a metaphor perhaps better suited to the frigid Soviet climate, it was snowballing. Only here, the people had to build the mountain, create the snow, and keep on pushing — all without ever being seen!

> *"Moshe received Torah from Sinai, and handed it to Yehoshua, and Yehoshua to the Elders ..."*
> Since the dawn of the Jewish destiny, Torah wisdom has

been handed down from one generation to the next. Indeed, the very word for heritage, *mesorah*, has its root in "*limsor*," to hand down.

Under normal circumstances, this process of handing down is a generational one: father to son, rebbe to talmid. But in the Soviet Union, beneath the shadow of the KGB, circumstances were far from normal . . .

✑ Passing It On

Eliyahu Essas was very proud of his first and youngest pupil, but his pride was tempered by fear for his future. Avigdor Eskin, seventeen-years-old, had been, in the parlance of the times, "turned on" to Judaism with remarkable swiftness. He attended every *shiur* possible, read anything he could get hold of, and made incredible progress. In his eagerness and excitement, he often forgot to take routine precautions against the all-seeing KGB; hence, Essas' fear for his safety.

Six months after attending his first class, Avigdor had a gift to present to his *rebbe*: his very own pupil! He had met, and taught, another young man, Lova Aivazov, later to be known by his Hebrew name of Aryeh. Lova was a remarkable student, even by the extraordinary standards of the movement, an *iluy* who within a year had gone from learning *aleph-beis* to study of *Gemara*, as well as *Musar* and *Hashkafah* *sefarim*.

Soon afterwards, Avigdor received the news: His visa request had been approved. He would be allowed to leave for Israel! This was no great surprise: The authorities often dealt with "troublemakers" by granting permission for them to leave! Naturally, Avigdor was thrilled at the thought of returning to a land he had never seen, except in his dreams. Still, his joy was tempered with sorrow at leaving his *rebbe* and, even more, his own *talmidim*!

But before his departure he, too, could grab a little "*nachas*." His *talmid*, Lova, was now a teacher himself, who could point to his own students. And later, when Lova received his visa, it was Reuven Kaplan, a close friend, who assumed the mantle of young leadership.

Thus, in the space of seven or eight years, one might find four "generations" following the Jewish tradition of *mesorah*.

A wedding in Moscow. The tiny apartment served as the "hall": the living room housed the chupah, the food, the dancing guests; the kitchen contained all the guests' coats, and served as the yichud room as well. Moscow's Torah network celebrated about thirty such chasunahs in the 1980's.

◆§ The Mysterious Student

Summer of 1981. Eliyahu Essas was riding the subway in Moscow, en route to a *shiur* he would be giving on the other side of town.

He looked around him at his fellow passengers. The usual lot: weary commuters, anxious students, a handful of drunks. Across from him sat a young man, a cap on his head, reading — could it be — a pirated edition of *Chumash Bamidbar*!

Essas stared intently at the young man and shook his head in disbelief. He had a good memory for faces and he knew, absolutely, that this young man had never attended a *shiur* of his. How in the world had he managed to lay his hands on one of his group's *Chumashim*? Even more puzzling, where had he learned a love of Torah, a love that was clear from the absorbed, dreamy expression on his face?

The next day, visiting the group's "summer camp," Essas told several of his *talmidim* about the strange encounter, carefully describing the young man. Sasha Bark, himself a student of Essas, exclaimed: "Oh him! He's a student of mine, he comes to my *Chumash shiur*!"

At that moment, a wave of exultation passed over Eliyahu Essas. He was no longer the "father of the *ba'al teshuvah* movement in Russia."

Now, he was a proud grandfather — with a network so far flung that a dedicated student could sit near him on a subway — a complete stranger.

> In 1973, Eliyahu Essas had opened his first Gemara. Four years later, he had realized his ambition of training a cadre of young people to lead classes of their own in Moscow. Finally in 1980, the network expanded to include other cities. Within two years, one could find a Gemara shiur in Leningrad, study parashas hashavua in Riga, eat kosher meat in Odessa. In cities as far away as Vilna, Minsk, Kiev, Charkov, Tbilisi, Vitebsk, Kuibyshev, Sverdlovsk and Kalinin, the word was out: Be a Jew. Learn Torah.

ᴥᔒ Moving On

Byelloruski Station, Moscow, Sunday night. A few drunks wandered aimlessly around, while others stared listlessly from the benches, exhausted by the day's revelry. Several men and women who'd spent the day cultivating their country gardens in nearby *dachas* sat quietly, buckets of strawberries and potatoes carefully placed on the stone floor beside them. A young couple proudly examined the bag of wild mushrooms they'd picked from a nearby forest. A bearded young man looked nervously at his wristwatch.

A train roared in. Among the alighting passengers was another bearded young man — Rabbi Eliyahu Essas, come to answer a call for help.

The call had come a few days earlier, from an engineer by the name of Grisha Wasserman, who had traveled to Moscow to meet Essas. As he spoke to the Leningrad resident, Essas was struck by a feeling of deja vu, an eerie sense that he was speaking to his own reflection. For this Wasserman, like Essas, was an observant Jew, self-taught, a religious product of an anti-religious society. And like Essas, now that he had learned the eternal message of Torah he burned to pass his knowledge on to others.

For hour upon hour, the two men walked the quiet streets of Moscow's Old City, as Essas shared with a rapt Wasserman the secrets of forming a Torah network in an ungodly regime. How to reach out to others — without drawing the KGB into the circle. What to teach to people who had to learn everything. How to get *sefarim*, funding, kosher food, *mezuzos*. How to run a *seder* and how to avoid arrest.

Grisha listened, spellbound.

The consultations, the trips between the two cities by various lecturers, the constant give-and-take bore impressive fruit: Within three years, more than one hundred people were part of Grisha Wasserman's Leningrad network.

> *Centuries before it had gained fame as the home of the incomparable genius, Rabbi Eliyahu, known as the Vilna Gaon. Its masters changed constantly — in three hundred years, it was claimed and conquered over and over again by the rulers of Lithuania, Poland, Russia, and Germany — but one thing remained certain in the city of Vilna: it was a city of incomparable Torah learning, a Jewish center known as the Jerusalem of Lita (Lithuania).*
>
> *The glory came to an abrupt halt, as the Communists annexed the city and brought with them their own warped brand of religion. Though a Communist education could not eradicate the memories and the beliefs of the older generation, Jewish youth in Vilna grew up estranged from its past, ignorant of its heritage, unaware of its obligations to a G-d it had never heard of. And so it remained, until a mathematician turned street cleaner, and a professional violinist, took matters in their own hands.*

ᴥᵴ Vilna Geniuses

Communist functionaries had obviously never heard of the advertising slogan that had made an impact in the capitalistic United States at that time: A mind is a terrible thing to waste. Thus, no one was overly disturbed when mathematician Zev Raiz was forced to take a job as a street cleaner. After all, hadn't Professor Raiz requested an exit visa from his homeland to live in the Zionist, imperialist entity? Didn't that clearly show that the man was either a fool, a criminal, or a parasitic ingrate?

Raiz's fall from glory had begun in the aftermath of the Six Day War when, like so many of his compatriots, he was electrified by news of the Jewish army's miraculous victory. By the early 1970s he and his wife, Carmela, an accomplished violinist who played with the Lithuanian

Symphony, were full-fledged refuseniks and the mathematician, summarily fired from his post, was delivering mail and, later, cleaning streets. When he wasn't involved in sanitation, Raiz kept himself busy writing, organizing, lecturing: the manifold activities of a dedicated dissident and refusenik.

In the course of his work, he met another refusenik, one Ilya Essas from Moscow. Because Essas' parents lived in Vilna, he traveled there and always would drop in on his friends the Raizes, where he knew he'd find a warm and friendly reception.

Over the years, the Raizes watched as Essas grew more and more observant. They were interested in, though cautious about, their friend's unusual life-style. They read the books he sent them, graciously hosted his students when they came to the city, even helped organize *shiurim*. At the same time they kept their distance, hesitant to make the final commitment to a Torah way of life.

And so things went, until the summer of 1982, when Zev and Carmela received a very special invitation. Rabbi Essas was running his summer camp in Riga and, for his friends, was willing to make an exception to an important rule: He would allow them to attend, though they did not live in Moscow.

For three days, the couple quietly attended lectures, read *sefarim* — and thought. Thought about G-d. Thought about the Jewish people and its destiny. Thought about Zionism, about Jewish history, about *mitzvah* observance and what it demanded. During a midnight walk in the woods, Raiz explained to Essas exactly what was going on. "We are not here to read another page in a book. From here, we leave as either totally observant Jews — or we do not give full Torah observance another thought."

Three days ... and the decision was made. Zev and Carmela Raiz would take on *mitzvah* observance as their forefathers had, a *na'aseh v'nishma* decision that would remain unshakeable through the long years of waiting.

In the Soviet Union, when the Communists held sway, the decision to live in accordance with the Torah was inevitably followed by the determination to teach others. So it was in Moscow, so in Leningrad — and so in that city of Torah, Vilna. The first step, of course, was to organize *shiurim* staffed, in the beginning, by young men — *talmidim* of Essas, until Vilna could provide its own homegrown teachers. The fledgling community received a boost when one of its members became a *shochet*, learning *shechitah* from visiting *shlichim*, and ultimately receiving *kaballah* from Rav Moshe Heineman of Baltimore. A three-year-long battle with authorities culminated in an unprecedented victory. In 1986, Vilna's *mikvah* was reopened to the public.

The glory that was Vilna could not be restored — but Torah had come back to the Jerusalem of Lithuania.

> *But while the parents were finally exploring the rich vastnesses of Torah, the children remained trapped within the atheistic Communist system of education. Can a parent break his own bonds and at the same time watch the fetters grow tighter around his children?*
>
> *After two years of teaching classes and training new teachers, it was the children's turn. Sunday mornings, when other Soviet schoolchildren slept late and enjoyed a day off, groups of young Jews would gather in a home for learning, ignoring the danger...*

◆§ *Partying*

Teaching Judaism to adults was bad enough. They could hound you out of your job, they could get you on charges of bourgeois activity, they could make your life miserable in a thousand different ways. But the risks and the dangers really began when you taught Torah to children.

Paragraph 142 of the Soviet Criminal Code explicitly forbade the teaching of religious subjects to any youngster under the age of eighteen. Breaking the law meant a three-year prison sentence. And everyone in that Moscow apartment on that Sunday morning knew it.

The apartment was a small one. In the living room, thirteen children, ages twelve to fifteen, sat around the round wooden table. On that table there was a bottle of Pepsi Cola, a plate of cookies — and a stack of notebooks. In the small bedroom another group of even younger children sat cozily on a bed, listening to someone tell a story. Four parents sat rather self-consciously in the kitchen.

The "teachers" in this very special Sunday school — most of them themselves recent *ba'alei teshuvah* — scrupulously kept up the pretense that this was merely a pleasant cultural activity. They had gotten particularly careful since a KGB visit to a class in 1981, during the crackdown on dissidents after the Moscow Olympics. It was during a pre-Chanukah class when the knock they all dreaded came: Six KGB men entered the room and ordered the dozen children present to stand against the wall, near the poster of *alef-beis* that hung there. "This is proof of anti-Soviet activity," one stated solemnly.

At that time, the children had gotten off with a warning and a good scare; now, even the youngest among them knew that words like "religion" and "school" were forbidden to be breathed.

The class in "History and Ethnic Traditions" went on. Suddenly the students heard an ominous sound: a knock at the door.

Everyone, student and teacher alike, was well trained. The children swiftly placed their notebooks among the other books on the shelves, and turned their attention to the refreshments. Would this be a repeat of the last KGB visit — and what would be the consequence this time? The door opened — to reveal another student, a latecomer. The group breathed a collective sigh of relief. The door was once again locked, the notebooks were brought out — and the lesson resumed.

Ah, summertime on the Black Sea! Cool ocean breezes, warm summer nights — and Torah!

‏ Camp Clandestine

The parents were learning Torah in Moscow apartments; the children were meeting for their Sunday school. But now summer was coming: summer, with its Russian tradition of taking off to the cool breezes of the sea. Children went to Communist camps heavily subsidized by the government, while their parents sunned themselves in Black Sea resort towns such as Yalta and Sochi, or Yurmala and Palanga on the Baltic, or the beach towns of Estonia.

And what of the small but growing cadre of Torah-observant — or at least interested — Jews? To send their children to Communist camps or to travel to resort towns meant risking the loss of all the learning gained at such great price during the year. In 1980, the audacious answer emerged: Start a clandestine camp for the children, and for their parents.

The first step was to find a place for the camp. Rabbi Essas tracked down a huge, two-story, century-old wooden house in the small town of Bykovo, forty kilometers outside of Moscow, a scenic village of lush forests and Russian alcoholics. The house boasted a lovely sun room made all of glass, no hot water, and an outdoor toilet. Its owner, a sharp-tongued septuagenarian by the name of Emma Borisovna, could

R' Essas in Bykovo. The beret was less likely to attract attention than a more traditional head covering.

boast of a physique almost as broad as the house she owned. Emma Borisovna knew a good deal when she saw one, and could drive a hard bargain: The cost of renting the ramshackle building was two thousand rubles for the summer, at a time when monthly rent normally ran to about four hundred. She was known far and wide for her sharp tongue; refuseniks who had stood up against the worst of the KGB quailed before her. Though Rabbi Essas was forced to pay her an additional two hundred ruble gift to stop her from screaming at the children, there was actually an important benefit derived from the camp's shrewish landlady: She effectively kept away all the curious local populace, which lived in deadly fear of her tongue lashings.

The clandestine camp's first season was a spectacularly successful one. In the first year, it boasted an enrollment of about fifteen children and ten adults, with twenty more adults coming in for weekends. Morning for the youngsters, just as in Orthodox camps throughout the world, would begin with *davening*. For many, this "beginners' *minyan*" was their first encounter with prayer. A breakfast of cottage cheese, carrots, tomatoes, porridge, tea, bread and butter followed. The little ones then went to their *aleph-beis* class or arts and crafts, while the older students worked on *Chumash* or *Mishnayos*. Their "learning *rebbes*" were students of Rabbi Essas, young men such as Reuven Kaplan, Aryeh Aivazov, and Alexander Bark, who themselves had just begun learning not long before. There would be lunch, perhaps a long walk, or bathing in the lake in the afternoon — with the children in caps and their bearded teachers drawing some odd glances from the locals — and then more learning.

In the infertile alcohol-soaked soil of a small Soviet town, Torah flourished.

After two successful summer in Bykovo, Rabbi Essas decided to extend the "camp spirit" during the year, by running a once-a-week class for kindergarten students in the dacha outside Moscow that had been used for camp. Then, one bleak November morning, with Chanukah just around the corner, there was a modern-day version of the Hellenist attack on children learning Torah: a KGB visit!

·⊷ The KGB Versus the Kids

Twelve five- and six-year-old children sat around a table, enthralled. Their *rebbe* was telling them a story — and such an interesting one! All about Chanukah, and how the children learned Torah and played *dreidel* when the mean Hellenists came to find them out.

A knock at the door interrupted.

Hellenists. The modern-day equivalent.

The KGB.

Six or seven neatly dressed men walked inside. They lined the children up against the wall. One carefully photographed each of the children, while another just as carefully took down their names.

One of the agents walked slowly around the room, staring suspiciously at the posters that brightened the walls. A picture of a four-sided top, an eight-branched candelabrum. Clearly, he told the three shaken adults who were present, this was evidence of anti-Soviet activity.

After what seemed an interminable time, the KGB pronounced judgment. The children and their adult chaperones were ordered to immediately vacate the dacha. Should they meet again, they were warned, the consequences would be dire.

Rabbi Essas studied the incident with the KGB, looking for a way of avoiding dangerous surveillance. The Moscow KGB clearly saw them as a threat and was interesting itself closely, too closely, in their activities. Even if the KGB would forgive the obvious religious nature of their activities, they were unlikely to look away from efforts completely antithetical to the Communist way of life: This was a private enterprise, privately run, without interference from the state. The likelihood of trouble, should they continue their summer camp in Bykovo, which came under Moscow's jurisdiction, was high. After all, it hadn't been many years before that the children of Baptists and Pentecostal Christians, privately educated by their parents, had actually been seized by the State and taken from their parents. Could they afford to run such a risk, for the sake of Jewish education? Could they afford not to?

Rabbi Essas turned his mathematically trained, Gemara-honed mind to the problem, and came up with a neat solution — move out of KGB notice. As Muscovites up to no good in Moscow, they were clear targets. If they would move to another city, the Moscow KGB office would ignore them, because they were out of their jurisdiction. The local KGB office, on the other hand, was not likely to interest itself in the doings of out-of-towners: Leave it to the Moscow "Central" branch.

Like all good ideas, this innovation came with a price: In order to keep local KGB men out of the picture, Rabbi Essas was forced to minimize contact with local Jews. A heavy price, when one knows and feels he can help them. Finally, Rabbi Essas worked out a compromise: When local Jews showed interest, Rabbi Essas and his students met with them — after the summer was over!

And so, with his deep understanding of the bureaucratic mind, Rabbi Essas had found a way of building a safe oasis in a dangerous desert.

ৰৢ Riga Summers

Together with his wife, Rabbi Essas made the 600-mile railroad trip to Riga. There, they met up with Lev Naumovitz Bassin, a Jew sympathetic to his compatriots, who in addition possessed a remarkably avaricious streak. He was, says Rabbi Essas, pure heart — and pure greed — a fortuitous combination for Rabbi Essas' purposes. Quickly, the lease was signed.

One month later, in late May, forty people traveled up to Riga. At first two or three families sat together in each car, studiously ignoring each other. After a few hours, when all was deemed safe, the men quietly made their way to one car and began to study Gemara, while the women bunched together to discuss the complex domestic arrangements, which including "rail-lifting" of foodstuffs all the way from Moscow. It was quite a trick, getting those three-hundred-pound sacks of potatoes to Riga — but somehow, they managed. Camp was ready to begin!

Rabbi Essas' first stop in Riga was in the home of the city's foremost Jewish personality, Reb Gershon Gurevich.

~§ The Dubious Rav

Reb Gershon Gurevich was another of those individuals who, at great personal cost, had fought all his life to keep the flickering light of Torah from being extinguished in the Communist darkness. During the black years of the Stalinist regime, with the KGB after him, he had fled and lived for seven years in the remote mountains of Georgia. Even after his return to Latvia, he'd lived in concealment for three years, until it became safe for him to emerge from hiding.

Now, Reb Gershon *was* Torah in Riga. For half a century, he'd served as unofficial Rav of the community, giving *shiurim* to the other old men of the city. He had circumcised virtually every Jewish boy in Riga. When meat was available, it was Reb Gershon who did the *shechting*.

It was for his capabilities as *shochet* that Rabbi Essas was now approaching Riga's venerable Rav. There were forty people, he explained, all of them needing kosher food. Could the Rav help supply them with meat?

Reb Gershon stared at the young man, shock and disbelief clearly marking his face. Forty young people — young people! — young people who'd been educated under the Communist rule, young people who had never seen the glorious days of Reb Meir Simchah and the Rogatchover — young people who not only seemed familiar with the terms of *kashrus*, but who sought kosher food to eat! Preposterous! Impossible!

Half a century of life under the Communists had taken its toll. Reb Gershon's wonder soon turned to suspicion. What manner of plot had the KGB hatched now?

Uncertain of whether he was dealing with a joker, a lunatic, or a dangerous informer, Reb Gershon indignantly refused the ludicrous request.

One month later, as Reb Gershon sat teaching *Mishnayos* before *davening* to eight elderly men, he heard noise, a lot of noise, and the sound of the *shul* door opening. Over half a lifetime of Soviet life had heightened his sense of danger, and he looked up, his heart beating fast.

There in front of him stood thirty or so men, fathers and sons, none older than thirty-five. The men had full beards, the boys and their fathers all had their heads covered with caps. Clearly, religious — clearly, tourists.

Reb Gershon and his *talmidim* approached the group to wish them *shalom aleichem*, find out who they were and what Western country they were from — and perhaps get some foreign cigarettes. Suddenly, they stopped, electrified. One of the bearded men was asking, in perfect Russian, if he and his group, natives of Moscow, could join their services!

As part of the decision to keep themselves uninvolved with local KGB, Rabbi Essas had until now determinedly kept a low profile in Riga, avoiding all contact with the small Jewish community. But today was special: One of the "campers" was becoming *bar mitzvah*. They had planned the day for weeks, a day of Torah learning, songs and celebration. The *bar mitzvah* had expressed a special desire to get an *aliyah* in a "real" *shul*; hence, the unexpected visit.

Reb Gershon's eyes were glued to the unbelievable sight of a younger generation expertly winding *tefillin* straps around its arm. Here, then, was living proof of the eternity of Torah. His sacrifices had not been in vain.

The tears coursed down his cheeks, as he wished the boy *mazel tov*.

At the beginning of the program, only about one-third of the participants were observing the mitzvos. How do you run a program to teach Yiddishkeit to children — and their parents — who know next to nothing? With patience... and Torah.

ᴥᔑ First Activity: Learning!

The day began in the thick Russian forest with calisthenics. The youngsters *davened* — some for the first time ever — and then split up into groups by age for their classes. Learning was interrupted in the morning for a dip in the Baltic; afterwards, it was resumed until lunchtime. Afternoons, again, were devoted to *aleph-beis*, to *Chumash*, and to teaching the fundamental laws of Judaism.

For the adults, there were *Gemara shiurim* in the morning, classes in *Tanach* and *Chumash* from four to seven in the afternoon, and another *Gemara shiur* from nine to ten-thirty p.m. Then, at eleven, began what was for many the highlight of the day: Rabbi Essas' *shiur* in the *sichos mussar* of Rav Chaim Shmulevitz. Using photographed copies of Rav Chaim's *sefer* (photocopying was strictly regulated, and unauthorized photocopying was punishable with up to five years' imprisonment), the participants would sit and discuss *hashkafah* and *mussar* topics until the wee hours of the morning, generally ending their talk with a walk under the clear, starry sky. In one summer, they learned through an entire year's worth of Rav Chaim's discourses.

The climax of the summer was a festive *siyum*. One year it was *Succah*; the next, *Beitzah*; and the next, *Rosh HaShanah*. The pain of imminent separation was forgotten on that day, as the participants rejoiced fervently in their newfound knowledge. Every youngster who had learned the *Gemara* said a *d'var Torah*, to the delight of relatives, friends and carefully chosen guests.

The results of these efforts? Although there might be two or three dropouts at the beginning of the summer, of those participants that remained through the entire program, every one without exception returned to his home determined to observe the *mitzvos*!

It wasn't only the KGB you had to worry about when you ran an illegal Jewish camp in the Communist republic of Latvia. There was the local police as well.

◦§ Police Encounters

If the people's spiritual needs were taken care of by contraband copies of *sefarim*, by dedicated *rebbeim*, by patience, perseverance, and a hefty dose of *siyata d'Shmaya*, what about their physical wants? How does one feed close to fifty people living in a benighted Latvian town where all foodstuffs are scarce — and still keep a low profile?

The area around the camp was not of much use. The men took turns foraging, carefully going through a five-mile radius around the town in search of milk and other staples, carrying their booty back to the camp in homemade rickshaws. Still, it wasn't enough, and to solve the difficult problem of provisioning the camp adequately, Rabbi Essas arranged for adults using the camp to bring with them potatoes, vegetables, and legumes. It was on one of those provisioning trips that the group's first run-in with the local police force took place.

When you're *shlepping* a huge dirty sack of potatoes, you don't dress up. And after a long, arduous train journey from Moscow with that sack, you don't look your best. You look, in fact, dirty, disheveled, and a general mess.

When Rabbi Essas' "delivery man," Reuven Piatigorsky, arrived at the railroad station, he looked terrible. So terrible, in fact, that the local police thought he was a hippy. Unfortunately, just days before, a group of Soviet hippies had held an illegal conference nearby. Assuming he was one who had escaped their net, the police promptly arrested him. For good measure, they arrested Mrs. Essas, who was awaiting him at the station, as well.

It was only after hours of accusations, denials, statements, counter-statements — and a lot of whispered prayers — that the misunderstanding was sorted out and the pair was allowed to return safely home, to camp.

This was not to be the only run-in with the local police force. When refuseniks Mark and Leah Tchernobrodov and their son drove up from Vilna, they took a wrong turn and ended up in the center of the city, on a street closed to traffic during the busy summer months. What in a free country would end up with a traffic citation could have, in this case, meant serious trouble.

The policeman who pulled them over immediately demanded their

Some of the Riga campers, summer 1984. The car belonged to the Tchernobrodovs, who took the wrong turn in Riga. All the children pictured here now live in Eretz Yisrael; most are in yeshivos.

destination. Sharlotes Street, Tchernobrodov reluctantly admitted.

The policeman, who turned out to be a fiercely nationalistic Latvian who loathed the Russians, smiled. "Oh, the Jew camp," he said, with a wink to a fellow nationalist. "You can go on. No problem."

> *The police, many of them fervent nationalists, were sympathetic; the neighbors, however, were not.*

⋙ *Pioneers Versus Jews*

It was a large, well-tended estate, and only a fence separated it from the camp. The youngsters learning about their illegal Jewish heritage stayed far away from their neighbors, though. For next door was a camp for Pioneers, the Communist equivalent of Boy Scouts. Every morning, they could hear the daily litany of young Communists — the singing of the Soviet national anthem, "The Indestructible Union of Free Republics."

For a month the hardy young Communists ignored their neighbors with their strange ways. Then, on the eve of the seventeenth day of *Tammuz*, a hail of stones came over the wall. The men in Rabbi Essas' camp clambered over the fence, but the perpetrators had vanished into the forests of the estate.

The attack was repeated a few nights later. Then, on the 9th day of *Av*, came another barrage of flying stones, the worst ever. "A real intifada," remembers one participant.

Something had to be done. At the fast's end, several of the huskiest men taking part in the camp paid a visit to the Pioneers. Some of the Russian counselors began to approach them, mumbling their usual catchwords: "Jewish Zionists, traitors..." Ignoring their baleful glances, the men approached the Pioneer camp's director. The man, a Latvian, seemed impressed by their veiled references to nationalistic ambitions. He seemed just as impressed by their less subtle declaration, "Stop them or we'll break some bones."

Whether it was sympathy for their cause or fear for his own physical safety that won the day is not clear. The attacks ended, and they never heard from their neighbors again.

In Latvia, observance of Jewish ritual was fraught with difficulty — with one exception. It was easy to mourn.

✑ Mourning and Basketball

It was *Tishah B'Av*, and all the "campers," adults and children alike, took part in a solemn journey through the former site of the Riga ghetto.

In the ghastly days of Nazi destruction, this ghetto had a special claim to fame. This was the only "ghetto without walls"; the fierce anti-Semitism of the surrounding gentiles ensured that no Jew would try to escape its misery and degradation, and thus no fence was ever erected to keep its imprisoned Jews inside.

Now, there was no marking, nothing to commemorate the crimes perpetrated here on the Jewish people, nothing to remind anyone that the Jews had some special connection to the area. A lovely landscaped park sat on the site of the former *shul* — and no plaque marked it. Verdant forests grew in places where thousands of Jewish martyrs had perished — and no plaque marked it. Here were Jewish houses, taken by non-Jews and now their property, without a ruble of compensation ever paid. Here was the Jewish hospital, unused and unmarked. The children stared somberly at a tiny crevice between two attached houses, listening as their *rebbe* told them how Jews had stood in the crack, motionless for days, in a futile attempt to escape Nazi notice. For many of the children this was the first mention they had ever had of the Holocaust, of the fate of the Jews during the Nazi onslaught, for Soviet policy had long been to ignore the Jewish ordeal. Though Soviet propaganda often spoke of the "Great Patriotic War," Hitler's war against the Jews simply did not exist.

Later in the afternoon, they returned to Yurmala and arrived at a large, modern sports center. This, they were told, had been built on the site of a *shul*, where Jewish summer vacationers used to daven before the War. Exploring the basketball court, they discovered the outline of a *magen David*, painted over. On one wall, there stood a closet filled with exercise mats; it had been, they realized, the *aron kodesh*.

Silently they left the building. In a quiet cul-de-sac nearby the group sat on the floor and said the *kinos*. Somehow, remembering the destruction of the Temple was easy as they sat there on the cold stone pavement.

Summer's end. How do you measure the success of the camp season? In the Catskills, you look at the spirit of the children, at the color war results, at the parents' comments. In Riga, success was measured by a different yardstick. Success was Zev Raiz, who later gained fame as the longest-held refusenik and as the "father" of the movement in his native Vilnius, who first accepted mitzvah observance in camp. Success was forty-year-old Valentin from the region of Kursk, who heard about the camp from relatives and came for a two-week stay. By the summer's end, he had committed himself to gradual mitzvah observance, and returned home to teach the 5,000 other Jews of Kursk. Success was Alexander and Arthur and Sasha and all the other young people who, inspired by an intense summer of learning, went out to form classes in their hometowns in Russia, Lithuania, and Latvia. Success meant the formation of groups of young educators, capable of changing one man's dream into a vibrant reality.

By this yardstick, the summer had been a monumental success.

⊸§ Goodbyes

And now it was over. The *siyum* had been celebrated, the farewells tearfully said. The joke making the rounds reflected the participants' shared feelings of accomplishment and hope, together with the cynical pessimism that permeated their lives: Next year in the Middle East — Jerusalem; or the Far East — Siberia.

There was one final challenge: transporting sixty people, including children, from the "free Jewish republic" they had managed to create for a summer, back to Moscow.

Fifteen families make a lot of luggage. The women and children took a local train to Riga, the closest large city, while five men boarded a large truck, obtained through the judicious use of bribery, in order to transport the luggage to the main railway station, where they would join their families.

The truck brought them to the station, where the men received several unwelcome surprises. First, they discovered that the luggage could only be unloaded on a platform far from the one where the Moscow-bound train was scheduled to stop. Second, there was no sign of their wives and children, who were to help them unload the truck and get the luggage ready for boarding to Moscow.

It was 6:10. The Moscow train was scheduled to arrive at 6:40, and would leave promptly twenty minutes later.

There was no time to worry about their families, no time to worry about anything at all. Desperately, the men raced to and fro, to and fro, bringing the unwieldy, heavy boxes from one platform to the next. By 6:30 — no sign of their families. At 6:45, arriving almost simultaneously with the Moscow Express, a local train chugged in, bearing the women and children. Two previous trains had simply been canceled, with no explanation.

The women rushed to their husbands — and saw, to their consternation, that though the Moscow express had just arrived, much of their luggage still remained platforms away.

More trouble — there was only one small door on the Moscow train through which they could load the luggage into their car. As the men raced wildly to get the remaining boxes, the women pushed, shoved, and jammed the boxes onto the car.

Seven o'clock. The train, with vacationers returning home, was ready to pull out. The women and children of the camp had gotten on — but much of the luggage remained to be stowed. And what luggage — precious books (some of them "illegal" photocopies) and kosher utensils. A treasure!

The train began to move. Rabbi Essas, desperate, hit the emergency brake. Forget the one door we are supposed to use and put the luggage anywhere on the train, he instructed his followers. And so these Jews, who spent a summer living quietly, trying desperately not to draw attention to themselves, proceeded to "occupy" the train, jamming luggage everywhere and anywhere, whether or not their tickets gave them the right. The train began slowly to move again; once again, the emergency brake was pulled and it screeched to a stop.

The police were beginning to get interested: What were these goings-on, here on the Moscow Express, flagship of the Latvian rail system? The place was chaos: police shouting "Hooligans!", conductors and trainmen yelling at each other, and, all the while, Rabbi Essas and his "campers" scampering along the platforms, loading boxes.

At last, just as the police began to approach their car, Rabbi Essas gave the signal: Release the emergency brake. With a wheeze and a roar, the great train lurched forward.

And now they had to face the irate conductors. By law, they should have faced fines and possible jail sentences. But by dint of jokes, pleasantries, some explanations, and judicious bribery, the authorities were finally placated. Everyone let out a sigh of relief, order was restored — and the Jews of the "camp" came together for one last summer *shiur*.

For some, the return to Yiddishkeit was as simple as finding a class, a rebbe, a sefer. For these fortunates, the words of Torah were like water to the thirsty, answering a deeply felt need with satisfying haste.

For others, though, the journey to observance was more circuitous. Again, we turn to Sasha, the musician whose curiosity about things Jewish had been piqued by the matzah of Pesach.

Sasha's Tale II: Hear, Oh Israel

Sasha's interest in his Jewish heritage grew stronger after that first *Pesach*, when he had seen thousands of Jews come together to celebrate a holiday. He connected up with a fellow Jewish student, a guitarist by the name of Alik, who invited him to join him in front of the *synagoga* for the upcoming festival of *Rosh HaShanah*. Though he had no idea of the holiday's significance, and though his parents begged him not to risk expulsion from school by making himself so conspicuous, Sasha readily agreed. Now, instead of gazing at the circles of joyous dancers as he had six months before, Sasha found himself in their center.

Fortunately, this time Sasha escaped KGB notice. However, he did come to the attention of Mila, a young woman who had recently begun to live an observant life. "We need a musician for a Jewish band," she told Sasha. Though this was clearly an illegal activity, Sasha was interested. Mila gave him the address of her teacher, Lova (who later become known as Aryeh) Aivazov, a student of Rabbi Essas now in his early twenties. Intrigued, Sasha decided to visit this Aivazov and see what he was up to.

Seventeen-year-old Sasha knocked hesitantly. The door was immediately opened by a young man wearing a strange knitted cap on his head. The man put a finger on his lips, motioning to Sasha to keep silent.

Wordlessly, the man gestured to a chair, offering it silently to his puzzled visitor. He then picked up paper and a pencil and began to write: "Shalom. My name is Lova. Would you like to take part in a *Purim shpiel?*" He went on to write that the walls were bugged. If the KGB heard Sasha's voice and identified him, he could get into trouble. If he had no wish to take part in illegal activities, he could leave now and no one would be the wiser.

Purim shpiel. Strange words — Sasha had never heard of them. Still, the offer appealed to his teenage sense of adventure — as well as the eternal sense of Jewish self-sacrifice bequeathed to him by his forefather Yitzchak. He indicated his agreement.

That was the beginning of Sasha's contact with the Torah network. He began to visit Lova on Friday nights, enjoying the strange sight of professors and engineers and students sitting around a table, singing Hebrew songs. He and his friend Alik decided to learn Hebrew. Both combined an interesting mixture of idealism and ignorance: Alik, particularly taken by the idea of Jewish observance, told his friend that he had decided to keep meat and milk separate. Then, shyly but proudly, he took the creamy *smetana* off his hamburger, put it on his plate next to the meat, and carefully ate first one and then the other.

One Friday night, after a particularly long dinner at Lova's house, Sasha arrived home. His eyes sparkled mischievously as he approached his mother, who was drying the dinner dishes. "Tell me, Mama, what would you say if I told you I believed in G-d?"

The dish went crashing to the floor, shattering into a hundred pieces.

Sasha, penitent, assured his mother he was just joking, just kidding around. He had just seen some people who actually did believe in G-d, and he thought it was a good joke.

Two weeks later he realized with a start that the joke was on him. He was an atheist no longer. He, too, was a believer.

Still, the road from belief to observance was a rocky one for the high-spirited teenager. Having learned of the *mitzvah* of *tefillin*, Sasha decided he wanted to try it for himself. Rabbi Essas sent him to Reb Sholom, a venerable old *sofer* who lovingly made *tefillin*, despite his age and illness. Reb Sholom handed him a pair and told him that though they were very expensive, he would give them to him for free. "Only see to it that you wear them every day."

And he did — for a week. But he had trouble getting those straps to wrap around properly, he forgot Reb Sholom's careful instructions, and, embarrassed to ask a second time, he eventually gave up on their use.

Davening was a similar story. In his initial enthusiasm, he'd asked his teacher, Lova, for prayers to say. Since his Hebrew was rudimentary, Lova had taught him just one line: *Shema Yisrael, Hashem Elokeinu, Hashem Echad* — Hear, O Israel, the L-rd is our G-d, the L-rd is One. "Just say this morning and night, Sasha," his teacher counseled.

Again, he began to practice. But one morning he woke up late and didn't even remember *Shema* until the afternoon. One evening, exhausted, he fell into bed, *Shema* going unsaid. After a short while, his prayers were forgotten in the rush of a busy, fulfilling life.

Other setbacks followed for the young man who had chosen to serve his G-d but had no idea of how to do it. His teacher, Lova Aivazov, received his exit visa: a "penalty" often offered by the authorities to young people they felt were growing too influential. At a party given by refuseniks for the lucky one who had been granted permission to leave, Sasha heard Rabbi Essas speak. Determined that he would take the place of his departing mentor, Sasha went to Archipov Street, near the synagogue, the very next Saturday night. Here, Sasha knew he would be sure to meet fifteen or twenty refuseniks, including Essas.

Eagerly, the teenager approached Essas. "I want to learn," he said.

Essas looked at him coldly. "So go and learn," he said. And then he abruptly turned away.

Sasha, insulted and hurt, left the street. Only years later did he learn the reason for Rabbi Essas' surprising reaction: Essas saw a known KGB informer standing right near them, and hoped, by his noncommittal reply, to keep young Sasha out of trouble.

Still, if there were obstacles and pitfalls and missed opportunities, there were great strides as well. One Sunday, when Sasha was eighteen years old, he nervously made his way to the Moscow Synagogue. There, he was met by seventy-five-year-old Reb Getzl Vilensky and several others.

With hardly a word between them, the men filed out of the synagogue. They split up, and at intervals of about ten minutes took several different cabs, on several different routes, until they arrived at their common destination, an innocuous-looking apartment in a residential area of Moscow.

Inside, a man was standing near a table placed by a window. He was a doctor, a professor who specialized in open-heart surgery. Dima Lifliandsky had come especially to perform today's operation — Sasha's long-delayed *bris milah*.

As Sasha waited for the doctor's preparations to be concluded, a mixture of impatience and apprehension on his face, Reb Getzl spoke with him. "Sasha," he asked, "why do you want to have a *bris*?"

"Because I am a Jew," Sasha replied somberly.

"Do you keep the *mitzvos*?" Reb Getzl asked him.

"I would like to," Sasha answered. "But it is hard, very hard."

"Do you keep kosher?"

Sasha did not reply.

Reb Getzl stared at him for a long moment. "Sasha," he said, "when you eat a piece of *treife* chicken — don't suck the marrow from the bones. Don't eat it until the bone."

Sasha understood the compassionate man's message: You can't do it all at once, but you must begin. A great weight lifted from his heart — and, from that moment on, he began to be more and more careful about the laws of *kashrus*.

During the circumcision, as he heard the men repeat the words *"b'damayich chayii* — you shall live with your blood," Sasha remembered the first time he'd heard the words. He'd been walking with Lova Aivazov, and his teacher had told him of prophecy, of the prophets who had spoken G-d's words to the Nation. These words, spoken by the *Navi* Yechezkel, had made a particularly strong impression on Sasha.

And then, just as his road to observance seemed to be becoming easier, the final blow fell. Sasha and his friend Alik were drafted into the army.

Chaim Briskman, a *talmid* of Rabbi Essas who had taken over Lova's position as Sasha's teacher and mentor, urged his pupil to follow Alik's lead and avoid the army service that would make *mitzvah* observance almost impossible. There was only one way for a healthy young man to get out of the draft: Plead insanity. It wasn't that difficult, really, and several newly religious Jews had done it. You had a family member report your alarming symptoms. You were placed in a psychiatric hospital for observation. And then — you simply lived an Orthodox Jewish life. You stood by a wall three times daily, shaking back and forth. You put boxes on your arms and head. You refused the nutritious hospital food and subsisted on vegetables. With such anti-social, not to mention neurotic, behavior patterns, there wasn't a psychiatrist in the Soviet Union who wouldn't certify you as unfit for army service!

With his new found religious fervor, Alik had convinced the authorities of his insanity in little more than a week. But Sasha hesitated. His parents begged him not to take the step, one which would certainly end his promising career as a musician.

A mother's tears are strong weapons. Sasha acquiesced to his parents' wishes, bid a sad farewell to his teacher and fellow students, and joined the Soviet army, a musician in a regiment band.

It was in this unlikely milieu that he was to make his final unshakeable commitment to *Yiddishkeit*.

Sasha loathed army life. He knew many of his fellow musicians from his years in the Conservatory. As civilians, they had been a cultured, likable lot. Here in the army, fighting over the best pieces of meat and guzzling vodka whenever they could find it, they seemed to him like animals.

And there was Dmitri, a giant of a man, an athlete with the build of a bull. He was a vicious anti-Semite whose greatest pleasure was provoking any Jew he came in contact with. His mother, he told Sasha once, before he found out that he, too, was a Jew, had been a washerwoman for a Jewish family. "She hated the *Zhids*, and I hate them even more," he declared.

Besides Sasha, there were two other Jews in the unit. One, Grisha Katz, came in for Dmitri's special attention. Grisha was a talented musician who played oboe, classical guitar and piano. He was a university-trained archaeologist whose myopic gaze looked out at an army life he was ill equipped to handle. He often declared to Sasha that he was a Russian, not a Jew. In his desire to find acceptance with the other soldiers, he would bring them sausages, help them with their duties. His efforts were in vain, however — the anti-Semites in the army detested him and did everything in their power to make him miserable.

One day, when Sasha was passing by the unit's soundproofed rehearsal hall, he heard some kind of commotion. Entering, he saw Dmitri shouting foul words, his huge hand upraised, ready to come smashing down on Grisha's bespectacled, terrified face.

Without a wasted thought or motion, Sasha deftly grabbed Dmitri's arm and flipped him over.

Now he was up on his feet, his hapless prey quickly forgotten. Dmitri stood next to Sasha, his face contorted with rage, and his bulging, scarlet eyes gave him the fearsome look of an enraged bull.

When he spoke, he did not shout. The hatred, the venom in his words carried them through the soundproofed walls and lifted them through the air into the ears of the soldiers waiting outside with bated breath.

"*Zhid*. Cursed *Zhid*. In one month I will be out of this army. My friends will come and kill you. You will wallow in your own blood. You will live in your blood."

The words struck Sasha like a blow. Here was the ignorant, bestial *goy* mouthing the words of the prophet that he had heard from his *rebbe* in another lifetime. It was as if G-d had sent Dmitri as His own special messenger, to remind an erring Jew of his obligations. *You will live in your blood. B'damayich chayii.*

Dmitri's hatred filled Sasha with astonishment and wonder. This man hated Sasha, hated his parents, his friends and relatives, his unborn children; he would do his all to destroy his entire people.

The thoughts flew through his head, even as his enemy staggered away. "I can protect myself, with my fists, with my rifles. But this will not end my danger. There are a thousand Dmitris waiting to destroy me and the Jewish people.

"G-d gives every animal a means of protection. A skunk protects itself with its vile smell; a deer with its swiftness; a lion with its terrible strength. Mankind protects itself with its brains and its weapons.

"And the Jew? G-d gave him the greatest protection of all — Himself."

In this strange, uplifted mood, Sasha strode back to his room. He felt he must somehow talk to Hashem, give Him his thanks and his prayers.

He remembered a *siddur* given to him by a friend before his army service began. Though he'd never used it, he had carefully secreted it in his bunkhouse. Now, ignoring the curious stares of his fellow recruits, he unearthed it and took it out behind the bunkhouse.

Reverently, he opened the brand-new book at random and carefully recited the words before him. *Shema Yisrael, Hashem Elokeinu, Hashem Echad.*

He stopped, thunderstruck. These were the very words his *rebbe* had asked — nay, begged him to recite each day!

He quickly closed the *siddur* and opened it up to a different page. The words staring out at him seemed to have a life of their own.

Shema Yisrael, Hashem Elokeinu, Hashem Echad.

A great awe came over him. Once again he closed and reopened the *siddur*. He almost expected it — again, the words of *Shema*.

First through an ignorant Russian peasant, then through the pages of an unused *siddur* and the words of *Shema*, repeated in *Shacharis*, *Ma'ariv*, and before going to bed, Hashem had sent Sasha a clear message, an urgent summons back to the heritage that he was in danger of losing.

From that moment on, Sasha's commitment to his G-d was unwavering. And he never missed his twice-daily recital of *Shema*.

The story did not end there. One more overt miracle awaited the young soldier.

With his decision to reinforce his connections with Jewish observance, he made contact with his former mentors in Moscow. He desperately wanted to join in some communal Jewish activity, to again feel a part of his people.

The next holiday, some four weeks away, he was told, was *Purim*. And the day before *Purim* was *Ta'anis Esther*, a fast day for the Jews.

Sasha's mind was made up. No matter what the cost, he would join his fellows in *shul* on the fast day.

Normally, the Soviet army would grant its soldiers leave only on Sundays. Ignoring the fact that he was going against a strong unspoken tradition of army life, and making the ultimate military error of calling his superiors' attention to himself, Sasha asked for leave during the week.

To his shock, it was granted.

The young man spent the entire day of *Ta'anis Esther* with his religious compatriots. He fasted, for the first time in his life. He felt a glorious feeling of unity with his people that he had never before experienced.

Too soon it was over, and he returned before nightfall to camp.

His fellow soldiers surrounded him. "It was a miracle you were gone, a miracle!" they shouted.

The story soon became clear. Dmitri, now discharged, had arrived at the camp completely drunk, armed with a razor-sharp knife, looking for his enemy. He and two drunken friends had spent the morning raging through the camp, seeking Sasha, bent on vengeance and mayhem.

Like the Jews, saved from the pitiless hands of Amalek in the merit of their fasting and penitence, Sasha's life had been spared because of his observance of *Ta'anis Esther*.

> *Sasha's tale is peculiarly dramatic, the stuff of cinema and novel. For most of the men and women who took on the mitzvos under the Soviet regime, the circumstances were much more mundane — but the choices just as difficult.*

◄§ Leah's Story

Leah Levin is a quiet, soft-spoken woman, a Soviet immigrant living in Jerusalem. Other than the fact that her head is kept covered, she is hardly recognizable from among the thousands of Russian-speaking individuals who have arrived within the last decade. The story of her family's discovery of *Yiddishkeit* typifies that of many of the *ba'alei teshuvah*.

In the 1970s, the Levins were a young couple struggling, not always successfully, to make ends meet in their Moscow apartment. Igor was a designer of scenery for theaters, Lena a teacher in a nursery school.

With regard to their Jewish heritage, the Levins were, perhaps, just a bit more advanced than most of their Soviet compatriots. They knew, and openly acknowledged, their Jewishness. They would sometimes attend synagogue, not out of any religious belief, but out of a desire to feel a connection with their people. They had a Jewish encyclopedia in their home, left to Leah by a grandparent. It sat, unread, on a living room shelf. And they had a long time friend, Moshe Pantilat, who kept telling them about some man he'd met who was having a strong influence on his life. The man's name, Moshe told them, was Ilya. Ilya Essas.

Not much. But enough.

In 1983, a Zionist connection invited Igor to work on a *Chanukah* play, helping to create the scenery. Intrigued, Igor agreed to join up. After one rehearsal, he got a phone call. The KGB was on the line, politely suggesting that he drop the project. He did. And that should have been the end of it.

But it was not. It was, though the Levins could hardly know it, only the beginning.

After giving up his one fling with Zionist activity, Igor and his wife, Lena, felt an unexplained emptiness in their lives. It had always been upon them somewhat, this dreary ache, this dull yearning for something they could not define. But now it seemed inescapable, a giant chasm that occasional visits to a synagogue could not hope to fill.

The Levins cautiously opened their encyclopedia.

Igor read the entry on the Sabbath. Every seventh day, it appeared, Jews had traditionally ceased working, in accordance with G-d's fourth commandment.

Strange words and concepts these: Sabbath, commandment, G-d. Strange, yet compelling.

The Levins took a long, searching look at their lives: Igor, so often on the road, traveling from theater to theater, city to city, in a ceaseless search for hard-earned rubles; Lena, left alone in Moscow, wondering what on earth they were struggling so hard for. Both of them searching,

searching for meaning, for purpose, for explanations of their universe and their lives.

It was a foolhardy notion, a ridiculous idea. But soon, for no fathomable reason, the Levins had made their decision. They'd never heard of the concept of *melachos*; indeed, they were unfamiliar with *matan Torah* itself. But, with the words of a secular encyclopedia ringing in their ears, the Levins gave up working on the Sabbath.

With their *Shabbos* now a free day, the couple became regulars at the Moscow Synagogue. It was there that they heard of a *shiur* given by a man named Essas, the one their friend Moshe had been so enthusiastic about. They decided, somewhat hesitantly, to attend.

It was spring of 1985. The lecture was a long one: a two-and-a half-hour discussion on a Jew's purpose in life. It was sprinkled with strange names and ideas — Adam HaRishon, Avraham Avinu, Moshe Rabbeinu. The Levins found it difficult, erudite, complex — and a revelation. It marked, for them, a complete turnaround in their lives. Before, they had taken a few hesitating steps into an unknown direction. Now, they knew exactly where they were going — to Torah.

After the speech, they shyly approached the Rabbi. Sensing their commitment, Rabbi Essas immediately said he would visit them at home. At the end of the visit, he invited them to join him in his summer camp in Riga. The Levins gave up their jobs in order to attend. There was no looking back: Their commitment was absolute.

Igor and Lena — now Yisrael and Leah — have traveled far from Moscow since that day, seen many new sights, met many new people. But, they insist, nothing, not even their first *Shabbos* in Jerusalem, can compare to those balmy Riga days. The unity, the hours of shared work and shared dreams, and, above all, the learning — the *shiurim*, the *sefarim*, the Torah — made an indelible impression. When Leah lit her first *Shabbos* candles, she shared her joy with twenty other women, many, like her, "first-timers." When Yisrael sang his first *zemiros*, he felt like a man who has carried a load for so long he almost forgets his burden — until it is lifted and he can stand up, straight and tall.

With summer's end they returned to their small Moscow home. Their neighbors eyed them suspiciously: Where had they been? What had they been up to? Leah's favorite tree, planted next to her door, was vandalized. The Levins didn't care. They had their *shiurim* to attend, their *mitzvos* to learn and observe. And, with their application for a visa, they now had a dream of freedom to cherish.

The dream became a reality a year and a half later, when they nervously boarded a Vienna-bound flight. This, some may argue, was the beginning of freedom. But the Levins will disagree. Their freedom had its start in a dacha in Riga. Or, perhaps, during a long lecture in Moscow.

Or even in the pages of a Jewish encyclopedia.

CHAPTER 5

The Perils

In 1976, a group of refuseniks known as "kulturniks," because they believed that until full-scale Jewish emigration became a reality there should be efforts made to strengthen Jewish life in the Soviet Union itself, decided to hold an open symposium on Jewish culture in the Soviet Union. The symposium was scheduled for December 19, 1976.

For a while, the KGB stayed out of the preparations. Then, in mid-November, its agents decided to take an interest...

Evening in the Essas apartment in Moscow. The children were preparing to go to sleep in their bedroom, while in the living room their mother went over some materials for the upcoming symposium. Their father, refusenik Ilya Essas, was working on an underground newspaper, a *samizdat*, that he edited, and was speaking to Tala Gurfel, wife of a friend from Estonia, human-rights activist Bennor Gurfel, who'd dropped by for a "working" visit — to pick up some books and other materials on Judaism and *aliyah*.

A knock at the door broke the peaceful silence. Essas opened it, and in stepped a group of men.

The KGB had arrived.

There were two uniformed policemen whose sole function, Essas knew, was to promote fear. Along with them to the search came two younger men, the "civilian witnesses" that were mandated by Soviet law. These witnesses were KGB trainees themselves. And, finally, the three truly dangerous men: men in their thirties, clean shaven, immaculate in business suits and ties. One of the smartly dressed men politely showed Essas his search warrant. They were looking for anti-Soviet literature.

The procedure was neat and orderly. Lock the door. Pull out the telephone wires. Fan out through the apartment. The witnesses watched, bored: They'd seen this before.

One of the plainclothesmen smiled at Essas. "I see you have children," he said pleasantly. "We'll begin with their room, so they can quickly get back to bed."

Essas smiled back politely at the man he knew was his deadly foe.

They began their search at 8 p.m. By eleven, they had just finished going over the children's room. They checked beneath floorboards, pulled open every drawer and closet. Later, in the kitchen, every package of rice and sugar was gone through with a knitting needle. Nothing was missed.

It was when they reached the living room, though, that they began to enjoy themselves. Here was a treasure trove: *samizdat* materials, literature prepared for the symposium. And books! Such books, so many books. Clearly subversive.

As the pile of books destined to be confiscated grew higher and higher, Essas grew more and more frustrated. Luckily, they didn't touch his *sefarim* — in 1976, the KGB couldn't dream that such arcane, old-fashioned books could pose any danger; it wasn't until the 1980s that they took any interest in Hebrew-language books. But they were piling up most of his Russian-language library!

He noticed one book that had been carelessly placed on the heap. "Six Million Accuse," it was called, an account of the Eichmann trial.

Essas turned to the investigator. "Do you want me to call AP or Reuters tomorrow, and tell them that the KGB looks upon the trial of Hitler's Fascist commander as anti-Soviet activity?" he asked.

The investigator, confused, stopped his work. "Perhaps not," he shrugged, placing the volume safely on a table.

Essas, sensing victory, pressed his advantage. "But you've taken all my books! Perhaps there are others that are not anti-Soviet!"

The investigator began to sweat. He wasn't used to being challenged, wasn't used to being unsure of himself. After conferring with a colleague, he returned to the pile of books and began a careful look at every single item.

In the meantime, the tiny apartment was growing more and more crowded. At about ten, Vladimir Furman, a refusenik, and Vladimir Albrecht, a human-rights activist, both friends of the Essases, dropped by to enjoy a Russian custom: a steaming cup of tea and heated talks around the table. By Soviet law, anyone entering a home during a KGB search may not leave until the search is complete — not even the dog Furman had on a leash! No one could call to let his wife know where he was — outside contact was forbidden and, in any case, the telephone had been disconnected. Everyone stood in the crowded kitchen, watching the proceedings, drinking hot tea.

By one in the morning, the search had ended. Now came the KGB investigator's moment of glory. He sat down next to the pile of papers, letters, and documents, and began to carefully list them. For each document, he would write a careful description: "A letter written on a yellow paper, with blue ink, approximately 10 x 15 cm." Then he would write the words with which the letter began, and those with which it ended. That was a prescription of the law — and the KGB never broke the law.

As he was compiling his list, Albrecht surreptitiously scribbled some words on a paper. He slipped the note to Essas, ostensibly worried that the KGB officer would notice it. The officer — excellently trained — saw it, and, naturally, confiscated it immediately, adding it to the pile of previously confiscated materials.

Finally, the KGB investigator picked up the paper and added it to his growing list. "White paper, lined, black ink, 5 x 12 cm. 'I firmly believe that. . . G-d exists.' "

Albrecht and Essas could hardly keep their faces straight. They'd had their quiet revenge for this night — the thrill of knowing that, possibly for the first time, they'd gotten a KGB man to announce the existence of the Almighty! That was an example of both courage and humor, and in what circumstances!

At seven in the morning, the KGB men politely said farewell, and drove off into the morning sunlight.

> But the KGB was not so easily finished with Essas. He and his colleagues were up to something — and they would find out what it was!
>
> Two days after the search, Essas received a sinister-looking red paper in the post. "Essas, Ilya is hereby summoned by the KGB Department of Investigations as a witness in criminal case number such and such, under paragraph 191 of the criminal code."
>
> Once again he was to face off with the Soviet Union's most powerful organization. Their weapons were shadowy rumors,

fear, and the omnipresent threat of prison. In Rabbi Essas'
arsenal was his faith — and a unique line of defense named
for, of all things, fruit.

⊸ P.L.O.D. Power

Because so many witnesses had been called for that day, the KGB's main office in Lubianka Square, near Red Square, found itself overloaded, and, as ordered, Essas appeared at a district office instead. The office he finally found himself in was a quiet, somber one with only portraits of Lenin and Brezhnev to break the dim gloom of its dull grey walls. The investigator, KGB major Bryantsev, was also a dim, gray sort of man, dressed neatly in a suit and tie. He had a pleasant, vacuous smile, and looked like nothing worse than an overworked, underpaid minor clerk.

Essas knew better.

After some preliminary greeting, the investigator began to shoot questions at Essas. With a calmness born of faith in Hashem, Essas drew upon a strategy developed by his friend Albrecht two years before. It was called PLOD — fruit, in Russian — and consisted of four lines of defense:

P — *Protokol* (everything has to be finalized in written form)

L — *Liechnoe* (to discuss only things related to your activities and not self-incriminating)

O — *Otnosheneye k delu* (only things related to the criminal case)

D — *Dopustimost* (morally permitted)

The strategy worked like this. First, Essas told the investigator that though he was perfectly willing to cooperate where the law requires, he would only do so if both the question and his answer were written down, *protokol*. The purpose of this strategy was to place a block between the investigator and the one being questioned in order to grant a psychological respite.

The investigator immediately agreed to Essas' request. The first victory had been gained.

Next, Essas announced his second rule — *liechnoe*: "I will not incriminate myself. If any information you ask for is self-incriminating, you must find it out yourself."

Reluctantly, the investigator agreed.

Then came the cream of the defense, *otnosheneye k delu*. "All questions must be related to the criminal charges under discussion, and nothing else. You are seeking information regarding anti-Soviet activities. If you question me, your question must be clearly related to such activity. As a loyal Soviet citizen, I will try to answer your questions — but only in this matter."

With this, Essas accomplished a two-fold purpose. First, he had closed off many difficult areas of interrogation. When the investigator asked him where he'd written his articles, Essas countered by demanding that he prove those articles were anti-Soviet. Even more important, he placed the burden of proof squarely on the shoulders of the KGB.

The last defense, *dopustimost*, allowed Essas to show a little moral one-upmanship. I will not incriminate another, he declared. I have taken a moral stand — I am different from you people.

By carefully adhering to these four principles, Essas managed to get through nine hours of interrogation. More than once, his interrogator threw his hands up in despair. "What can I do? I can get no information from you!" At this point, he turned confidential and appealed to Essas' better nature: "Have pity, my superiors will be furious." But Essas remained adamant.

If P.L.O.D. was his weapon, it was faith that was his strength. Even as he fenced and parried and exchanged pleasantries and veiled insults with his interrogator, Essas knew that the danger was real and was imminent. He would leave his office intact, that was clear. But whether or not he would ride the subway home, or be taken in one of the KGB's black Volgas to prison, was a question that remained unanswered.

Promptly at six, the interrogator dismissed him. For today, at least, he was free.

This was not the last encounter Rabbi Essas was to have with the infamous secret police. In December 1980, after three years of quiet religious activity on the part of the network, the KGB decided to attend one of the now famous shiurim.

⊸§ The Knock on the Door

Thursday evening in the Moscow apartment of Lova Aivazov. The year was 1980. Forty-five young men had just ended a *shiur* in *parashas hashavua*. Still to come, after a short break, would be a lesson in *Tehillim*.

Nine p.m. The cookies and samovar had just been produced when there was a knock on the door. A latecomer no doubt, come to enjoy the second half of the class.

The door opened. There was no latecomer there, grinning shyly. There was only the KGB.

About sixteen people entered the small apartment: five uniformed policemen, ten plainclothes KGB officers, and one woman from the Moscow District Council.

The woman pounced delightedly upon the books piled neatly on the dining room table. "Illegal activities," she shrieked, grabbing the books and scooping them into the capacious handbag she had brought just for the purpose. Through the haze of the first shock, Rabbi Essas could not help but compare her to a hungry Moscow shopper who'd found a rare hoard of chickens in a store.

But his irreverent thoughts quickly flew back to the situation at hand. The KGB men, clearly in charge of the situation, had begun checking the internal passports of each of the participants, carefully noting down their names, addresses, and places of employment. The first to be arrested would be anyone who lived outside Moscow who had not obtained the proper permit to be in the capital overnight. Rabbi Essas' eyes swept over the group — *b'chasdei Hashem*, tonight there were only Muscovites in attendance.

But as he gazed at his students, he saw increasing signs of fear and some panic. Rabbi Essas, too, felt afraid — but only of one thing: Perhaps this was the end of the Torah network he'd created in the heart of the Soviet Empire. Later, other fears arose, but at this moment he could think of nothing else.

His first task was to calm his students. But it was forbidden to talk to each other until the end of the KGB "Operation." Rabbi Essas had a message to give his students. But how could he talk to them of *bitachon*, of faith in Hashem, here, under the eyes of the KGB?

He took a deep breath and approached the KGB agent who was clearly in charge of the operation. "You must do your job here, and I cannot change your mind," he said to him in a voice loud enough to be heard all throughout the apartment. "But remember, first of all — our people existed for 3,000 years before you — and we will live long after yours have ceased to exist. Second, such names as Yagoda, Ezhov, Beria — all of them were heads of the KGB — and all of them, today, are gone, killed one by one by their successors. Do what you have to do — but do not be arrogant before us."

The KGB agent's face was a mask of granite. But Essas hadn't really sought to elicit a reaction. He had wanted to send a message to his students, encouraging them to continue to be strong — no matter what.

The message got through. Faces lightened, hope replaced fear. And after the scare was over, after the interrogations that took place within the next two weeks, 43 out of the 45 people who'd been in attendance continued to come to classes and study Torah, though in a reorganized format — in smaller groups, reshuffled each week to another place.

> Other than that one raid, and one other that followed it almost immediately, the Torah network that was growing in Moscow found itself strangely untouched by the foul KGB hands. Individuals did get their share of interrogations, scares, midnight visits, and refused visas, but as a group they seemed to have been left quite alone.
>
> Years later, a former member of the Moscow Synagogue dvadtzka helped explain the special protection they had had.

◄§ A Few Madmen

A KGB agent in Moscow had just received disquieting news. A refusenik, already known to their office for his emigration activities, had begun a class in, of all things, the Jewish Bible and Jewish laws. It was a small class, obviously, but did it pose a threat to the Soviet State? That was his job to decide.

The thing seemed outlandish, a holdover from a past so remote that it hardly seemed worth bothering about. Still, it had to be looked into.

The agent searched for a pen, and began to write.

Not long afterwards, the president of the Moscow Synagogue received a letter. It was ostensibly from the State Committee on Religious Affairs; the president knew better than that. The KGB was making inquiries.

"We have been informed that a group of young people are coming together to study Jewish law. What is the synagogue's evaluation of the future of such an endeavor?" it read.

The answer was simple, and quickly penned. There is no danger in these activities, the president assured the "State Committee." Judaism is a religion of strict observance, and the laws are almost impossible to keep for young people in the Soviet Union. Students, for instance, must attend University on the Jewish Sabbath. The Soviet diet, too, is already quite restricted, and no one would voluntarily restrict it further by keeping the laws of *kashrus*.

"This will end with three or four madmen who can't do any harm to our state," the president assured the Committee.

As a result of the letter, the KGB let the classes continue, unharmed. And by the time they realized that "three or four madmen" can turn into hundreds of observant Jews, the network had turned into a movement,

had gained momentum, and had become so well known that it could no longer be destroyed.

CHAPTER 6

The Cost of Mitzvos

The ba'al teshuvah in the Soviet Union had a long and arduous, and often dangerous, road to travel. First, he had to learn and understand that he was a Jew. He had to cast off the bonds of atheism that the State had woven so tightly around him. He had to recognize his G-d.

After he'd made that extraordinarily uplifting leap into belief, though, the journey was not yet over; in fact, it had hardly begun. Yiddishkeit is not a religion of belief, it is a way of life. Torah cannot merely be learned, it must be lived, it must be translated into action — the action of mitzvos. But how do you keep the mitzvos in a restrictive, totalitarian state that has vowed to eradicate such behavior?

◆§ A Trip to the Butcher's

The *Rosh HaShanah* holiday was approaching. The religious Jews of Moscow, as did their brethren throughout the world, closely scrutinized their deeds, the first step towards true *teshuvah*.

At the same time, just as Jews everywhere do before a holiday, they turned their attention to their larders as well. *"Ein simchah elah b'vasar u'v'yayin,"* our Sages say: "There is no joy without meat and wine." Wine could be pressed from raisins right there in their homes, but where was the close-knit Moscow religious Jewish community to find meat for the holiday?

A few years earlier, procuring kosher meat had posed no problem for Jewish Moscow: The supply was more than adequate for the almost non-existent demand. Reb Mottel, an elderly Moscow *shochet*, could get

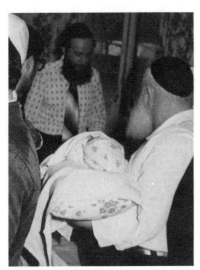

Reb Mottel served as Moscow's mohel as well as its shochet. At the bris of R' Essas's son, David, 1978, Reb Mottel is standing at left.

his hands on a piece of livestock from the local peasantry about once a month. He would *shecht* the animal, hoping that no *sh'eilos* would arise: because there was no rabbinical authority available to *pasken*, only *glatt* kosher animals were acceptable.

If the animal was satisfactory, Reb Mottel would cut the meat in the tiny area behind the Moscow synagogue that served as the butcher shop and distribute the proceeds to all those interested in kosher meat. In the 1970s in Moscow, that added up to about fifteen or twenty retired old men and — much to everyone's astonishment — young Ilya Essas.

But now, a decade later, much had changed. The animal that had served a dozen now had to be shared among over one hundred people. For all of his efforts, Reb Mottel could supply Moscow Jewry with two to three pounds of meat a month for each family — and that included the bones. Not much to face *Yom Tov* with.

Since Reb Mottel couldn't handle the demand, the religious Jews of Moscow found another supplier. Five times yearly, Reb Gershon Gurevich, elderly Rav of Riga, would *shecht* animals. For a few extraordinary days, someone's home would be turned into a factory, as the meat was *kashered*, smoked, and formed into long, pungent, hearty sausages.

With *Rosh HaShanah* on its way, a messenger was duly dispatched to Riga to get the delivery. This was no easy job — some four hundred pounds of frozen meat and fresh sausages had to be hauled in valises from Riga to Moscow; only the railroad would do. The fifteen-hour ride back to Moscow was the stuff of low comedy and horrifying nightmare. The messenger tried to act casual and ignore the strong, almost overwhelming smell of garlic. His fellow passengers, jammed together in the stuffy train, hurled insults and abuse; some, their taste buds tantalized by the powerful smell, actually tried to steal the meat.

Finally, the meat, and the tired messenger, arrived at the platform. Now there remained the problem of transporting it to a central distribution point. There were no porters, and taxi drivers took but one sniff and moved on. Sometimes the weather reached minus thirty-five degrees, and yet the messenger sweated, as he pulled his load up, and down, and up again, through the station.

Despite the hardships, the meat finally reached its distribution center, where it was swiftly packaged. Calls were made and, within one day, everything was given out. Moscow Jews would celebrate their *Yom Tov* in class — with goulash, and those pungent, luscious sausages!

Meat was only one part of the menu — and only one part of the problem. Imagine Yom Tov without fish...

৵ A Fish Story

R' Essas sets out on an early morning "shopping trip" for kosher meat and fish.

The building was an old and dingy one, in need of repair. The electric light in the lobby had burned out years ago, and no one had ever bothered replacing it. The darkness, though, was a blessing: it concealed the peeling paint, the filthy floors, and the two men engaged in their illegal activities.

They spoke in monosyllabic whispers, these two suspicious-looking men. One, bundled up against the freezing weather in a shabby, much-patched gray overcoat, his fur hat pulled low over his bloodshot eyes, carried a battered suitcase with him. He handed the suitcase over to his younger co-conspirator, a man wearing a fur cap and sporting a beard. The bearded man opened the valise, wrinkled his nose as he glanced inside. With a nod of approval for the merchandise, he then wordlessly exchanged it for a small envelope. The shabby man ripped open the envelope, quickly ran calloused fingers through the wad of rubles, gave a quiet nod. The two disappeared into the Moscow night.

Contraband? Stolen goods? A drug deal?

Fish.

With meat such a difficult luxury, fish had become the mainstay of the kosher Jew's diet. But with the food shortages that characterized Soviet life, a supply of kosher fish couldn't be guaranteed. To ensure a good supply, Rabbi Essas — the bearded conspirator in the dark hallway — recruited a cadre of peasants who worked in fish-packaging plants. These men, most of them alcoholics, learned from the "Jewish priest" all that was necessary — what kinds of fish were permitted to the Jews, what *simanim* had to accompany them. After a while, they became familiar with the Jewish calendar, knowing when the order would be enlarged because of a *Yom Tov*. Before the summer, they would bring hundreds of pounds of fish, to be frozen and transported to "camp."

The Jewish "priest's" rubles were happily taken, soon turned into vodka, and swiftly drunk. In return, a succulent carp graced that week's *Shabbos* table.

"And you shall write on the mezuzos of your home." To openly nail a proud symbol of Jewishness in a spot where anyone — neighbors, employers, spies — could see it, took a special kind of courage. The reward, at least on one occasion, was a special kind of hashgachah.

ᴅ§ The Indestructible Mezuzah

The Essas family, newly returned from two months in camp, stood in the small hallway of their apartment building. Their feelings were mixed as they surveyed the scene before them. During their absence, renovations had been made and, among other things, a fresh coat of brown paint had been laid on the walls, ceiling and doors. On the one hand, the walls finally looked bright and clean. On the other hand, the none-too-careful workmen had wreaked havoc doing the job. Whatever had gotten in the way of the paintbrushes — light fixtures, wall hangings, plants, tiles — had either been pulled down, broken, or painted over. The place was a wreck.

Rabbi Essas, surveying the carnage, gave a sudden start and bounded up the stairs. His *mezuzah!* He had put it up not long before, one of the first of Moscow's Jews to so openly display his allegiance to an outlawed G-d. He'd derived such satisfaction every time he saw this most visible of *mitzvahs*. (It had also proved an invaluable guidepost to *shlichim* searching for his apartment in the ill-lit hallways!) Surely the drunken peasants doing the painting hadn't spared his beloved *mezuzah*. What would he find when he reached his second-floor apartment?

What he found was a miracle. A small, unnoticed, minor miracle, perhaps, in the vast scope of world history, but for Rabbi Essas a clear and comforting case of *hashgachah pratis*. The workmen had gotten to the *mezuzah*, had ripped it down mercilessly in order to swab the paint on the door. And then — Rabbi Essas surmises — a workman had noticed the strange Hebrew writing on the little paper within. The symbols had aroused the latent superstition that dwells in the Russian peasant's breast. The *mezuzah* had been reverently replaced, completely undamaged, by some nameless, unschooled Russian peasant.

> *"And you shall bind them as a sign on your arms; and it shall be an ornament between your eyes."* But try explaining that to the Soviet authorities. . .

⋖ The Spy

Things looked grim for Valentin. A student in Moscow University, he'd been caught attending classes in Judaism. Now he was in trouble. Big trouble. Retribution was swift, and soon Valentin found himself expelled from the University's hallowed halls. He was now an able-bodied man without a University exemption, and there was only one place for him — the army.

Within weeks, Valentin had been drafted and shipped out to a small Siberian town, far, far away from *Gemara* classes, kosher food, and fellow Jews. All the *mitzvahs* that he'd so recently taken on had become impossible to observe. Valentin determined to hold on to one thing, at the very least. Every morning, he told himself grimly, he would put on his *tefillin*. No matter what.

It wasn't easy to drag himself out of his bed on the frigid Siberian mornings. And yet Valentin managed to be up half an hour before reveille, don his *tefillin*, and pray to his Creator.

One day, one of his fellow soldiers who had happened to waken early was astonished to see Valentin standing quietly in a corner, carefully winding straps around his arm, carefully placing a box upon his forehead. The next morning the soldier, his suspicions awakened, again awoke early, and again witnessed this mad — or possibly traitorous — behavior.

By the third day, the soldier had done his patriotic duty, and when Valentin roused himself from his all-too-short night's sleep, there were two officers on hand to witness these strange goings-on. The officers, both embittered remnants from Stalinist times, were not impressed with Valentin's protestations that the *tefillin* were religious objects. Prayer they could understand, although they didn't like it; but these straps? Clearly, Valentin was a spy, and the straps and box some sort of transmitting device.

Their first step was to confiscate the dangerous transmitter. Valentin, still protesting, insisted upon accompanying the *tefillin* to the lab where they would be examined. Curiously enough, the officers agreed, though insisting that a military guard escort him.

In the lab in a small Siberian town, the technicians had never seen such a device. The boxes, they surmised, served as transmitters, while the straps were antennas. As Valentin watched, horrified, they actually opened up the *tefillin* boxes. Gleefully, they pulled out the writing. A secret code! It is Hebrew, he protested. A language that has been dead for 2,000 years, they answered. A perfect code!

Getting more and more angry, and not a little scared, Valentin urged his captors to contact the small local Jewish community in the city of Novosibirsk to verify his words. The next day, the investigators duly visited the synagogue. They returned, unimpressed: No one had been wearing the straps and boxes. It was . . . Saturday.

Eventually the president of the synagogue heard about the hapless Jewish soldier and came forward to verify his story and explain that no Jew put on his straps on their Sabbath. The officers, not particularly eager to press charges of espionage, partly because it would look bad on their unit's records, and partly because they simply didn't want the trouble, were prepared to drop the charges. Instead, they told Valentin, he would be discharged on psychiatric grounds. "Because, if you're not a spy, you certainly must be crazy."

Instead of two years, Valentin finished his army service in two months, and soon was ready to rejoin his family and friends — Jewish friends — back in Moscow. Later, because he hadn't spent much time in the army, he was allowed to leave Russia and emigrate to Israel, without having to undergo the ordeal of being a refusenik. Valentin, now living in the Negev, knows where his "good luck" came from: his devotion to the *mitzvah* of *tefillin*.

> Remember Sasha, the young musician who took a circuitous route to Jewish observance? When we last left him, he had just been saved from death because of his determination to properly fast on Ta'anis Esther. But the tale of devotion — and of miracles — is not yet ended.

ᴥᶴ Sasha's Story IV: The Exodus

Sasha's narrow brush with death, and the amazing circumstances behind his escape from the brutal Dmitri, left him a changed young man. Enough of procrastination, forgetfulness, just plain laziness: He would be a Torah Jew and observe the *mitzvos* as best he could, even here in the Soviet army.

Following the counsel of his mentor, Chaim Briskman, the young army musician began to *daven Shemoneh Esrei* twice daily. This was no easy task in the rigidly structured Soviet army: Sasha awoke an hour before reveille, and stayed up for an hour after curfew, in order to pray to his G-d.

Sasha would not *daven* in the filthy surroundings of his barracks. But a sentry posted near his door made exit that way impossible, especially in the evening after curfew. How could he get away to pray?

Nothing stands before grim determination. Sasha found a small vent near the ceiling of his barracks, one he could reach from his upper bunk. Night after dangerous night, he would unscrew the vent and somehow wriggle through the tiny opening to get to the clean night air.

Though his evening ritual was never found out, the word got around that every morning Sasha was carrying on strange rites behind the barracks. Oddly enough, he was never punished for his breach of military discipline; indeed, he sensed a heightened respect for him on the base, a respect not accorded any of the other Jewish soldiers.

Not long after Dmitri's abortive murder attempt, Sasha realized with a start that *Pesach* was coming. *Pesach*, the holiday of Jewish national liberation, had special meaning to the young man, conscripted into an alien army. Nor had he forgotten that it was the *Pesach matzah* that had been the catalyst for his journey to observance.

Pesach was coming and Sasha would celebrate it properly — at a *seder* with other Jews!

The very idea was madness. In Sasha's brigade, overnight leaves were hardly ever granted, even under the best of circumstances, and Sasha's commanding officer, a Ukranian who served as the army orchestra's conductor, was a known anti-Semite who didn't entertain any cordial feelings for the young Jew. A request for such a leave would almost certainly be denied, and might even result in punishment for the foolhardy soldier.

I will do my part, and G-d will do His, Sasha thought. *I'm going to try it.*

Not long before the holiday, Sasha decided it was time to make his unprecedented request. He approached the door to his commander's office and raised his hand, ready to knock.

His hand was still poised in mid-air when the door flew open. There, before him, stood his commanding officer, dressed in traveling clothes.

"I've no time now," he barked at Sasha. "Go see Major Y—, he can take care of you."

Though his mien remained calm and respectful, Sasha's heart inside him leaped with joy. Major Y—, unlike his commanding officer, was a good-natured ignoramus who would grant almost any request when accompanied by the proper "documents" — a bottle of vodka. Sure enough, Sasha asked for — and received — permission for overnight leave.

Hashem had rewarded Sasha's *mesiras nefesh* by granting him a night off, a *seder* observed as it should be. But there was still more to come.

The *seder* had left Sasha uplifted and joyous. But now he was back, spending the first day of *Yom Tov* on his grim, cheerless base, forced by the Soviet army to play music together with a group of anti-Semites.

By mid-morning, Sasha's despair had jelled into an unshakable determination. Whatever the consequences, he had to spend the next *seder* with his fellow Jews again. He just had to! He would request another night's leave.

It was not a propitious time for such an outlandish request. His commanding officer had returned — today there was no good-natured assistant to ease things. If his C.O. hadn't already heard about Sasha's leave the previous night, he was sure to see it on Sasha's records, in the event that Sasha approached him for leave. Not only would his C.O. be angry because of the breach of military discipline, he would be furious when he realized that his assistant, and not he, had been the beneficiary of Sasha's bribe.

But Sasha had to try.

That afternoon, a competition was held between several army marching bands. Sasha's unit had not done well; as a matter of fact, they had the lowest score of all the contestants.

When the contest was over, the unit commander, furious, trembling with rage, addressed his soldiers. Each was commanded to play his pieces. If there was one error, if one note was off tune, the C.O. warned, the soldier lost all leave for a month.

One by one, the soldiers stood up in front of their enraged C.O.; one by one, they lost their leave.

Sasha was no exception. He did his best, but his best would not allay his C.O.'s fury: one month's leave canceled.

As he stood before his superior officer, Sasha wondered if he could find the courage, the determination, and the *chutzpah* to make his outrageous request. And then he remembered the Jews of Egypt demanding their freedom, stepping into water up to their necks, doing what they knew to be right and trusting to G-d to help them.

He saluted smartly and asked his C.O. for leave that very night.

His commander stared at him in disbelief. For a moment, he could hardly speak. Finally, he found the words — and they were hard ones.

"Get back to your barracks," he hissed. "Two months leave are canceled. And stay out of my sight — if I see you here on the base, I will make mincemeat out of you!"

Disconsolately, Sasha returned to his bunk. There, he carefully unearthed a *siddur* from behind a loose rock and began to say *Tehillim*. "G-d will answer you on your day of distress," said the psalm. Sasha sighed — surely, this had been his day of distress.

He had just finished the psalm when a soldier came to call him to the C.O.'s office. Sasha shrugged his shoulders stoically: What else did his enraged superior have in mind for him?

He stood at attention before his C.O., inwardly trembling, outwardly calm.

The major had just six words for him. "You may leave for the night."

There was no apology, no explanation. There was just the miracle of redemption, replayed for a Soviet Jew who wanted so badly to attend a *seder*.

Am Hasefer — the People of The Book. But what happens when the books are impossible to find?

❧ The World of Soviet Publishing

A *shiur* in the *mussar* discourses of Rav Chaim Shmulevitz is being held on a weekly basis. It is a popular *shiur*, drawing about twenty regulars. That means twenty *sefarim* needed for the participants.

How do you get them?

If you live in Boro Park, Baltimore, or Bnei Brak, you take a leisurely walk to the nearest *sefarim* store, ask a clerk which shelf to look at, charge it on your VISA or write a check, and watch as he wraps it and rings up the sale. If you live in a city with a small Jewish population, perhaps you ask a friend to send it to you, or you may pick up a phone and wait for a brown-uniformed UPS driver to deliver it to your door. You might use a catalog, or order it through your local *yeshivah*.

No problem.

But if you lived in Vilna, in, say, 1984, things were a little bit different. In order to get those twenty *Sichos Mussar*, you were forced to join the world of Soviet publishing.

Private printing presses were illegal in the Soviet Union. If they got you under Article 191, it could mean three years imprisonment; if you had broken the more serious Article 70, printing anti-Soviet materials, you could wind up in jail for seven to ten years.

With such severe punishments in the offing, private typesetting just wouldn't work. The equipment was expensive and bulky, and the illegal books could be used to trace their source.

How did you print your *Sichos Mussar*?

A *shaliach* from America came to visit. At Rabbi Essas' request, he brought him a copy of the *sefer*, which he "accidentally" left behind. In the same package, he brought a camera and as much film as he thought the authorities would let him get away with.

The *sefer* was brought to a darkroom — a makeshift affair, created in an alcove of a small Moscow apartment. Here, one found some antiquated developing equipment, all of it small enough to be cached away on a moment's warning.

Each of the *sefer*'s two hundred pages was carefully photographed. Then, just as carefully, twenty copies of each negative were printed. (With film and materials so hard to obtain, the "publishers" could not

*"Shiurei Da'as"
— a sefer
"published"
directly by the
Moscow Torah
network, 1984.*

afford to make more than one photo of a page; thus, on occasion, one
negative had to be used to print hundreds of copies!)

Twenty copies of a two-hundred-page book makes for 4,000 photos
that must be clandestinely developed on old, unreliable equipment.
When that difficult, and dangerous, task had been completed, the next
step in production began. Under the supervision of Aryeh Westfried, a
young student of Rabbi Essas who headed the "publishing department," a binding machine — so old that one suspects it may have been
used on Gutenberg's original Bible — was put into motion.

Finally, there was the problem of storage until a way of getting the
books from Moscow to Vilna could be found. Like every publisher,
these young Soviet Jews had a warehouse: in this case, the basement of
a small apartment building, hired from a drunken janitor who was kept
silent by the judicious application of bribe money and liquor.

When you opened the *sefer* you realized that it was not only the words of Rav Chaim that were going to teach you something. The smudged, sometimes illegible pages of the *sefer* itself contained a powerful lesson of determination and *mesirus nefesh*.

Keeping the mitzvah of taharas hamishpachah, going to the mikveh, was also not easy. It was only after he had already emigrated from the Soviet Union that Rabbi Essas fully understood the monumental sacrifice observing this mitzvah entailed.

◦§ Inconveniences

Not long after he had left the Soviet Union, in 1986, Rabbi Essas found himself visiting a middle-sized British city. The major topic of conversation within the Orthodox community was the need for a new *mikveh*. The city, it seemed, had two different neighborhoods with sizable Orthodox populations, but only one *mikveh*. Again and again, Rabbi Essas heard about the difficulties, the terrible inconveniences, and the problems the city's women faced in getting to the *mikveh*.

Though he sympathized with the women's honest concerns, Rabbi Essas could not help but think of his friends left behind in the Soviet Union. When he had begun to become observant, there had been just three working *mikvehs* in the entire Soviet Union — one in the Moscow synagogue, one in Leningrad, and one in Riga. The hundreds of *mikvehs* that had once been part of Jewish life had either fallen into total disrepair, or were used by synagogues or government bodies as warehouses.

Rabbi Essas thought of his *talmidim* in Kiev and Vilna. Their wives would go to the *mikveh* despite the tremendous inconvenience: a train trip of twelve hours each way. Those who lived near the sea would go into the water until the icy waves made it impossible. They fought the authorities as well: In Vilna, it took three years of haggling and arguing with government officials to get the old *mikveh* reopened.

In the mid-1970s, there were approximately five women in Moscow using the *mikveh*. By 1985 over one hundred and twenty women were keeping the laws of *taharas hamishpachah* — despite the "inconvenience."

By the mid 1980s, the once moribund Moscow mikveh was serving more than one hundred and twenty women. At the center of this hive of activity stood a short, stocky, elderly woman, possessor of a pair of shrewd eyes and an indomitable spirit.

✣ The Bubba

If Rabbi Essas can be called the father of the Soviet *ba'alei teshuvah* movement, Frieda Koronova deserves to be known as its grandmother.

The men and women who were returning to Jewish observance in Moscow, Riga, and Leningrad knew little about the elderly widow who served in the Moscow *mikveh*. She wore a kerchief, she lived alone in a small Moscow apartment — and she was there when they needed her.

As the network of observant Jewish families grew, so did the number of women determined to fulfill the precepts of family purity. The network spread the word: Contact Frieda Koronova. And so they did, in ever-increasing numbers.

At first, Frieda was suspicious. Was this a KGB ploy, or some kind of practical joke? But once convinced of the seriousness of these women's commitment, Frieda Koronova joyously joined the group.

Finding a place to hold *shiurim* was a continual challenge. Most people lived in small apartments, and there was simply no room to hold the increasing number of participants. Many of the students still lived with parents, who refused to countenance these strange, dangerous goings-on.

When Frieda heard about the problem, she set about to solve it by offering her own small place. From then on, she would sit in her miniscule kitchen, a beatific smile on her face, listening in on the learning that she couldn't understand a word of, beaming proudly at her "grandchildren." The *shiur klali* was held there for the most advanced students. Her small apartment near the Voykovskaya Station of Moscow's subway ultimately saw more *talmidei chachamim*, and heard more words of Torah spoken, than any other in the city. "*Dos iz mein gantz leiben* — This is my entire life," she once told a visitor from Israel who delivered a *shiur* in her home.

The young people got a taste of her indomitable spirit one evening, when their *shiur* was interrupted by a knock on the door. Police!

The little woman stood in the doorway, a bulwark protecting her loved ones, a fierce lioness protecting her young. "I went through

A shiur in "the bubba's" apartment. R' Moshe Eisemann, mashgiach of Yeshivas Ner Israel, gives a lesson in Divrei HaYamim, in Frieda Koronova's living room, 1984.

Hitler's camps. Fascists killed my entire family. These people are my only grandchildren. Hitler didn't kill me — and you won't kill me either."

In the face of such determined opposition, and perhaps with the memory of their own *"babushkas"* in their minds, the police shamefacedly turned away, to wait for their quarry downstairs, where it was "safer." Used to police ways, the participants simply climbed up to the roof, found a small crawl space, and made their careful way to the next entrance. Hardly glancing at the ominous black Volga parked in front of Frieda's apartment house they nonchalantly walked home, unspoken mixed feelings of triumph, anxiety, and gratitude in their hearts.

Such was the movement's "bubba."

When a Jew observes Torah, he is known by the proud title of "shomer Shabbos." It is Shabbos that, more than any other mitzvah, separates the Jew from the rest of the world. But how does a youngster observe Shabbos in the six-day school week of the Soviet State?

Red Saturday was coming, and ten-year-old Chaim had a problem.

For the course of the school year, his father, an observant *talmid chacham* heavily involved in the Moscow Torah network, had worked out an ingenious way of keeping his three children out of school on Saturday mornings. He had found a doctor, Dr. Lilia Yoshpe, a non-observant Jew, who had agreed to sign a note stating that the children suffered from asthma, and that treatment was available on Saturday morning only. This had been a courageous act on the doctor's part — if caught, she faced up to seven years imprisonment and the revocation of her license to practice medicine.

Despite the risks, and the teachers' doubtful looks, the scheme had worked fine, and none of the children ever attended Saturday morning classes. Now the question was — what to do about Red Saturday?

On the Saturday before April 22, Lenin's Birthday, all of the Soviet Union would join together in what the Communist slogan writers termed "the fight for peace." On that glorious day, every worker "volunteered" to do work in his place of employment, and donate his salary to the Soviet government. Normally, the government would "earn" close to one-half billion rubles annually in this way.

Students, too, were not exempt from "Red Saturday." They were expected to take part in a major cleanup and recycling campaign. To refuse to participate was a clear slight, an invitation to disaster.

So what was little Chaim to do?

As they gathered together in the morning, Chaim, who had trudged the three miles from his home to his school, joined his schoolmates. Volunteers were needed, the teacher in charge announced, to take charge of cleaning the storage areas — a dirty and difficult job.

Chaim immediately raised his hand enthusiastically.

While his fellow students outwardly hailed his patriotic fervor, inwardly many wondered at his stupidity in choosing such an unpleasant task. What they did not realize was that it had one distinct advantage: It took place far out of anyone else's sight — and thus, if he could not spend his *Shabbos* at a splendidly set table, with *zemiros* and *kiddush*, at the very least he could avoid desecrating his holy day.

Chaim was not the only child who went through such perils — and succeeded, thanks to the *mesiras nefesh* of parents, and people such as Dr. Yoshpe, and, surely, the Almighty's guiding hand. The Essas children, too, never once were *mechalel Shabbos* in all their years in the Soviet school system.

> Bar Mitzvah. *That unforgettable day when a young man finally grows up, takes responsibility for his own actions, earns the reward for his mitzvos and his limud Torah.*
>
> But in a place where mitzvos are unlawful and Torah study a sin — how does one celebrate?

⊸ In the Desert

When Yosef Essas was to be called to the Torah in celebration of his *bar mitzvah*, times were still very dark in the Soviet Union where he lived. In the interregnum between General Secretaries Andropov and Gorbachev, the Union was ruled by surly, threatening Konstantin Czernenko. Glasnost had not yet been introduced, and the tiny number of Jews who observed *mitzvos* did so at great risk, keeping a very low profile.

But Eliyahu Essas did not want to keep a low profile for the *bar mitzvah* of his eldest son. He was determined to celebrate it properly, making a *kiddush Hashem* that few would ever forget. His son would be called to the Torah. Publicly. In Moscow's largest synagogue (one of only two that had official sanction).

There hadn't been a *bar mitzvah* like this one in the synagogue in something like sixty years. But there would be one now, on *Shabbos Parashas Bamidbar*, the actual day of the *bar mitzvah*.

In some ways the preparations for the *bar mitzvah* in the Essas home resembled those that would take place in cities throughout the world. The young man was instructed, tested, drilled, and drilled some more in the correct *trop*, until the entire family felt they could recite the *parashah* by heart. Food was prepared. No caterers, no buffets or Viennese tables — the *kiddush* would include canned fish, lemonade and home-baked cakes: a feast indeed.

The biggest problem that faced the Essas family (with the exception, of course, of an unexpected KGB visit) was the question of weather. The month was May, a warm but often rainy season in Moscow. The walk to the synagogue from the Essas home was exactly two hours and fifteen minutes each way. Essas knew the time to the second — after all, in his last six years of living in Moscow he only skipped the walk four or five

An Essas family portrait, taken the day before little David's "upsherin."

times when the temperature plunged past minus forty, or when he was out of town!

A two-hour-and-fifteen-minute walk in the pouring rain was not a pleasant prospect. The Essases anxiously scanned the skies. Ominous rainclouds hung down low, scudding across the gray sky.

They set out. The usual route: down Leningradskoye Highway to Gorky Street, past Red Square. As always, Essas thought of the Bolshevik hero, Vladmir Lenin, lying dead in a mausoleum there, with a staff of scientists working feverishly in a three-story institution under the building, trying to keep his body preserved in its crystal coffin. Lenin was dead — and the Jewish heritage he had so despised lived on.

The weather held, and Rabbi Essas and his son (the other children, Esther and David, were too small for such a long trek and stayed home with their mother) proudly entered the *shul*. Tourists who had heard tales of religious persecution in the Soviet Union gaped in astonishment as they heard the young man carefully intone the words of the *parashah*.

Parashas Bamidbar. The elderly men who frequented the synagogue listened to the youngster's sweet, high voice, and could not help but think of the *midbar*, the desert that surrounded them. Many could remember the glory days of Judaism in Russia, Lithuania, Latvia, when *yeshivos* abounded, Torah study was beloved and respected, and the Jewish people, if impoverished and persecuted, still lived. But for this one *Shabbos*, at least, they could hear the words of Torah-proud Jewish lives. And now — the desert. The spiritual wasteland by a young man, a child born under Communist hegemony, educated in atheistic schools. Here in the barren desert, hope still grew.

The *parashah* was read, the cakes served, the last herring enjoyed. Now, it was time to go home.

The clouds, ominous before, now hung even lower and blacker in the sky. From the distance, Rabbi Essas and his son could hear the faint rumble of thunder. They increased their pace. The rumbling grew louder. They looked around, but saw no place to take shelter.

They had already reached their street when the first drops started to come down. As they opened the doors of their apartment building a huge bolt of lightning lit the dark sky. A crack of thunder — and the heavens opened, pouring down in drenching, freezing raindrops.

Safe at home, Rabbi Essas and his wife beamed with pride at their *bar mitzvah* boy. In this (very rainy) desert, their son had blossomed into something very special.

The clearest enemy of the Soviet State was the political organization. As a result, any gathering of more than three or four people was always suspect. But it takes ten to make a minyan!

A clandestine wedding ceremony, held in the kallah's apartment. R' Essas reads the kesubah, handwritten by a Moscow sofer, a talmid of R' Essas who'd received his kabbalah from Dayan Ehrentrau during one of his visits to Moscow.

◈§ One Saturday Morning in Moscow

David left his house on Ulbricht Street one Saturday morning. He shivered in the frigid Moscow wind, and pulled his fur cap down lower over his ears.

The city was quiet on this Saturday morning. He strode quickly through the streets, never glancing around him.

He'd walked for about a mile, when he noticed two young men chatting on a street corner. He passed them by without so much as a nod. After a moment or two, the men casually began to walk in the same direction. Neither had any idea of where their final destination would be: It was safer that way.

Another half mile up Leningradskoye Highway. Another man, this one bearded, waited on the corner. Again, without any sign of recognition, he began to saunter after the little group.

Finally, after picking up one more street-corner loafer David made his way to the apartment picked for that week. He knocked quietly, and wordlessly entered when the door opened. Minutes later, the two who had followed him repeated the knock; the fourth man, too, soon entered.

Inside sat six men waiting for the newcomers. The *minyan* was complete.

Davening with a minyan in Moscow was dangerous; finding a minyan in a remote Soviet prison camp was next to impossible. And yet — it was done.

◢§ Sasha's Story V: The Minyan in the House

As Sasha's commitment to Judaism deepened, his KGB file thickened. Finally, someone had enough of his oddball, Zionist, religious behavior. He was transferred out of his cushy Moscow unit to a tiny base in a bleak Soviet region used mainly for prison camps.

The punishment proved to be a blessing in disguise, though. No one could quite figure out what Sasha was supposed to be doing: He wasn't a prisoner, but he had no military function at all. He met up with two other musicians and formed an impromptu army band. His unofficial status gave him the freedom to truly deepen his commitment to Yiddishkeit.

He spent the first month on the new base fruitlessly looking for other Jewish soldiers. Finally, one of his comrades mentioned that he'd noticed a Jewish cemetery on the outskirts of a nearby town.

Sasha's joy when he finally found the modest graveyard was immeasurable. They might be in coffins but, dead or alive, they were his people! He almost hugged the stones that bore Jewish names here, in this town where he was so far from his brethren.

Suddenly he looked up and saw an elderly Jewish couple on the other side of the cemetery. He approached them with a smile, but they took one look at his Soviet army uniform and fled.

Disappointed, Sasha continued his walk through the cemetery. Soon he found a Russian peasant, half drunk, sitting nearby.

The man, who turned out to be the watchman in the cemetery, was a veritable fount of information on the Jewish community in the town. Yes, there were Jews in the town. And yes, they did meet on Saturday morning for their prayers.

That Shabbos morning, there was a hesitant knock on the door of a small cottage near the edge of town. The door was opened and then almost slammed shut again in the face of that most terrifying of images — a Soviet soldier. Only when the soldier quickly explained that he was

Jewish himself and that he wanted only to *daven* with a *minyan*, did the ten old men who had gathered there sigh with relief and allow him to enter.

The thrill he experienced when he was given an *aliyah* in this tiny hut in this remote Russian town has remained with Sasha as one of his most joyous memories, on a par with the moment of his arrival in Israel.

After *davening*, Sasha approached his hostess, an elderly widow who owned the house and allowed the semi-clandestine *minyan* to meet there each week. He was shocked to see her casually place a log in her woodburning stove.

Sasha was terribly curious: Why would a woman who was *mechalel Shabbos* publicly risk everything to have a *minyan* in her home?

The woman herself soon answered him. Her father, she told him proudly, had been the head of a local sausage factory during the dark days of World War II. Though there had been extraordinary famine in the region and the hunger had been intense and deadly, her father had refused to eat sausages that, in his position, he could have easily obtained. He gave them to his children and his wife, but he starved rather than eat *treife*.

Though he had been unable to transmit the *mesorah* of his forefathers to his own children, he had given them one precious legacy: the belief that a Jew sacrifices for his religion. Thus, in his honor, she gave her house for a *minyan*, despite the danger.

Succos is the time of rejoicing. But with the wind howling around you, and the sub-zero temperatures, and snow piled up on the ground, rejoicing outdoors is quite a trick...

⋙ Soviet Succahs

As with other visible *mitzvahs*, building a *sukkah* presented quite a problem to the growing numbers of Soviet *ba'alei teshuvah*. Most Soviet citizens live in apartments, and few have porches suitable for *sukkah*-building. Even those that did have room for a *succah* also had neighbors who would have protested had they dared to build the flimsy structure.

What to do?

For many years, the Moscow Synagogue had put up a *succah* for its elderly congregants. But until the mid-1980s, the synagogue authorities forbade its use by young people. In 1981 they actually called policemen to keep out the large number of Jews who wanted to sit within its four walls.

With the image of burly policemen blocking the entrance still clear in their minds, Rabbi Essas and his *talmidim* realized that they would have to do something else to celebrate *Yom Tov*. They hiked through a forest at the outskirts of Moscow, about two miles from their homes, and there, with only the trees to bear witness, happily built a hut to sit in for eight wonderful days.

Shabbos presented a problem, though: There was no *eruv*. But after some thought, they came up with a foolproof plan. The day before, on Friday, they carefully secreted a cache of food and drink within the *sukkah* ready for use on *Shabbos*.

The next day, as they approached their *succah*, they heard the sound of laughter. Slowly, nervously, they approached. Inside, they found four Russian peasants exultantly drinking down the vodka the Jews had placed there the day before! "Join us for a drink," one of the peasants roared hospitably. With no other choice, the Jews, resigned, accepted the peasants' hospitality.

The next year, a group of *ba'alei teshuvah* traveled to the dacha they had rented for summer camp to spend all eight days of *Succos* there. Excitement ran high: at last, the chance to enjoy a *Yom Tov* without the constant fear of being watched! Only one element marred their joy — the frigid temperatures and snowdrifts. Although they were halachically absolved from sitting in the *succah* because of the inclement weather, they refused to give in to such trifles as wind-chill factors, and happily sat, shivering, in their own *succah*.

One morning, as they were finishing a warm breakfast, there was a tap on the shaky wooden door. Police! Even here they could not escape the all-seeing eye of authority, the all-embracing fear that permeated their lives. The neighbors, it seemed, had filed a complaint against their illegal structure.

We are only enjoying a picnic, the Jews protested. The policeman in charge pulled his warm coat closer around him and eyed them skeptically. A picnic, in below-zero weather?

Though he let them off with just a warning, that was the last year they dared to build the *succah* in the dacha. The next year found them, once again, braving the snow and darkness of a Moscow forest, hoping that the wandering peasantry would not once again make themselves at home.

One of the first stops for many Soviet immigrants to Israel today is to a mohel, to receve a bris milah. But the ba'alei teshuvah who lived in pre-glasnost days did not want to wait for the day — who knew when it would finally come — when they would receive their visa to emigrate. And so they found other means.

◌৵ Heart Surgeon — With a Jewish Heart

During the week, Dr. Dmitri (or Dima) Lifliandsky was a respected professor of heart surgery, a skilled specialist who had achieved enormous success in the medical world.

On Sundays, he was a felon.

Every Sunday, this not-yet-observant Jew would travel to a different Moscow apartment, where he would hold his "office hours." For the next five hours, he would see up to ten patients, all suffering from the same complaint — the desire to enter into the Covenant of Avraham in a regime dedicated to wiping out their beliefs.

For five hours, the dining room table would serve as an operating table, the salon as a surgical theater. Using local anesthetics, Dr. Lifliandsky would circumcise adults and older children. (The babies were circumcised by Reb Mottel, Moscow's *shochet* and *mohel.*)

During the week, Dr. Lifliandsky would compound the felony by practicing illegal "private" medicine: He would visit each of his patients to make certain they were healing properly.

Had Dr. Lifliandsky been found out, had it been discovered that he was practicing private medicine, doing operations at home, and aiding and abetting in circumcising Jews, he would have, at best, been stripped of his right to practice. At worst, he could have faced criminal charges.

Disaster was one infection, or one informer, away. And yet, although he "practiced" for ten years, and circumcised thousands of men, the authorities never learned of his activities.

Though the KGB made observing those mitzvos between G-d and man particularly difficult, even bein adam l'chaveiro — obligations between fellow Jews — did not come easy in the economically strapped atmosphere of the Soviet Union.

ـۃ *Another Jewish Child*

The news was passed around in the Moscow Synagogue one morning in 1983. An elderly congregant had a friend, another elderly Jew, who had just undergone one of the worst tragedies imaginable. This man's daughter, the single mother of a four-year-old boy, had committed suicide.

To compound the horror, his four-year-old grandson, now an orphan, had been placed by the authorities in a Communist children's home. This elderly Jew had seen his daughter die a terrible death; now, he had to watch as his grandson's Jewish *neshamah* shared that dreadful fate.

Rabbi Essas, perturbed and anxious, immediately considered offering to adopt the young child, but he realized that given his lack of an official job and his status as a refusenik, there was no way the authorities would acquiesce. He was, after all, a highly suspicious character, almost a criminal. Would they allow a young Soviet citizen into his care?

When he next spoke with his *talmidim*, Rabbi Essas mentioned the sad story. Alexander, one of his closest pupils, immediately looked up in interest. He and his wife, Lena, were in their early thirties, living in a tiny Moscow apartment with their two young sons, ages four and two. They didn't have much money; they didn't have much room. But what they did have was a job — Alexander was a brilliant mathematician who worked in the computer field. Even more important, they had room, not in their apartment, but in their hearts. A Jewish boy had to be saved — they would do it!

The couple went through all the rigorous procedures necessary. Finally, the adoption went through, and Moshe became a member of the family.

And when Alexander and Lena moved to Israel in 1985, little Moshe, the Jewish *neshamah* saved form the Communists, happily accompanied his family to his homeland.

CHAPTER 7

Friends from Abroad

The decision to learn more about Judaism, to take the courageous leap into the dangerous unknown, was one that every ba'al teshuvah had to make for himself. After that, though, many found friends to help them along the difficult road: rebbeim, fellow students, old men who could still remember their cheder lessons, young people who had become observant under the Soviet regime, and, in later years, shelichim, men and women who would leave their secure, comfortable homes in Western countries to visit their beleaguered brethren behind the Iron Curtain, to teach — and, often, to learn — from them.

❧ Amos in Moscow

Erev Tishah B'Av 1973. Rabbi Pinchas Teitz, *Rav* of Elizabeth, New Jersey, was on a trip. This was no summer vacation, no relaxing or stimulating Rabbi's sabbatical. Rabbi Teitz was visiting the Soviet Union, long before the end of the Cold War, to see what he could do to help Jews there.

Rabbi Teitz, a venerable septuagenarian, was an unlikely pioneer, but this Latvian-born *Rav*, who had been a rising star in Riga in the 1930s and had been influenced by his personal contact with both Rav Meir Simchah of Dvinsk, the *Ohr Somayach*, and the Rogatchover Gaon, was indeed a breaker of new ground. In the early 1970s, few of the "establishment," both religious and non-religious, were making personal contact with refuseniks. There were relief activities, and a good deal of quiet diplomacy, but the idea of sending personal messengers

Rabbi Teitz
and Rabbi
Essas meet
in Elizabeth,
New Jersey.

to bring tidings, and help, from the Free World had not yet caught on.

But Rabbi Teitz was there in Moscow, looking to see how, and whom, he could help.

On a trip to the Moscow Synagogue, one young man came to his attention: a young man, for one thing, among these elderly Jews; and, clearly, a serious, committed, and bright young man. Thus, even at this early stage, Rabbi Teitz marked Ilya Essas as someone he wanted to meet.

Not that getting together was easy. The synagogue president, Efraim Kaploun, had strictly forbidden contact between the *yeshivah* students and foreign visitors. Thus, the elderly *Rav* was forced to meet this intriguing student outside, walking through the streets of Moscow.

Their first meeting, on *erev Tishah B'Av* 1973, was brief but memorable. For Rabbi Teitz, it was exciting to meet a young man who had accepted Torah on his own, even here in the Communist wasteland. And for Eliyahu Essas, meeting someone truly steeped in Torah knowledge, someone whose every word reflected Torah images and Talmudic knowledge, was nothing short of a revelation.

There were more revelations to follow. The two men met again the following year, during the fierce Moscow winter. They couldn't speak to each other privately in the synagogue — Efraim Kaploun saw to that. Essas was afraid to hold serious discussions in Rabbi Teitz's hotel room — contact with foreigners was just the sort of thing that would raise KGB eyebrows, and Soviet citizens were forbidden to enter tourist hotels. With no other choice, they walked through the frigid streets of Moscow. The temperature was minus twenty and the vapor formed swiftly around the mouths of the two men who walked so briskly just to keep their blood circulating.

It was not just the merciless wind that brought a rosy glow to Essas' face. He was hearing something new, something so exciting as to be almost unbelievable. They passed Dzerzhinsky Square, and Rabbi Teitz quoted Amos, a Prophet that Essas had not yet studied: "For days are coming. . . there will be not a hunger for bread or thirst for water, but rather to hear G-d's words." He then proceeded to tell of the strange new phenomenon in Israel and the United States that was just beginning to be called the *"ba'al teshuvah* movement." He told of men and women who had left their secular milieu to study *Gemara* in Jerusalem, of young people from totally assimilated families learning of the meaning of *Shabbos.*

Winter's icy fingers were forgotten; a great warmth enveloped the young man. For the first time, his own personal quest took on a world-wide significance. He was not alone, exploring a frightening unknown, taking an untrodden path to a hidden destination. He was part of a great world-wide movement of Jews, each following his own destiny, but each linked by a yearning so strong that it had been prophesied millennia before.

Not for the first time, a Prophet's words had brought comfort and inspiration in a far-flung corner of a cold, hard diaspora.

> *For the next few years Rabbi Teitz was virtually the sole contact that the growing community of Russian ba'alei teshuvah had with the religious world. He brought them precious gifts: hard-to-obtain sefarim; packets of brick-like charoses; and, especially important in the land of the ubiquitous eavesdropper, children's erasable tablets (you wrote down your "incriminating" comments, showed it to your co-conspirator, and then swiftly erased the evidence by*

picking up the plastic sheet!). Even more important, he brought news of a thriving Torah world outside the barred walls of the Soviet Union.

Six years later, more help came from the outside world, from a very different source.

☙ A Fateful Encounter

He was a red-headed businessman, a British subject who spoke the King's English with a decided German accent. He had spent his youth hiding from Nazis in a small Belgian village. As a refugee in England, he had gone to work at the age of fifteen. Now, Ernie Hirsch was a successful and respected businessman on holiday in the Soviet Union.

He had seen Ilya Essas' name on a list of refuseniks posted in a London synagogue and decided to look him up. What he found astonished him: an entire network of observant, learned Jews that had sprung up, seemingly out of nowhere. No one knew about them, there had been no publicity at all, and little help.

Ernie Hirsch was about to change all that.

His first job after his return to England was to spread the word of this phenomenon to influential *rabbanim* and laymen. He began to send *shelichim* to visit on a regular basis. Ultimately, two would arrive every other week. Among those sent through Hirsch's efforts were Dayan Chanoch Ehrentrau, SEED activist Rabbi Joe Grunfeld, Erwin Landau, who became a close friend of Rabbi Essas and his *talmidim*, and a good portion of the faculty of Gateshead Yeshivah. Hirsch — code-named "Gingy" by the refuseniks for his red hair — spread the word outside England as well, and soon a small but steady group of Americans, and Israelis with foreign passports — Rabbi Moshe Pindrus of Ohr Somayach, Rabbi Eliyahu Meir Klugman, and Rabbi Ezra Hartman — appeared at Rabbi Essas' door — or, more accurately, met him at a train station, in the front car.

But Mr. Hirsch's involvement did not end with sending others to teach and visit. He raised funds to send educators who could not pay their own fare, and to buy *tashmishei kedushah* for the Soviet Jews. He personally briefed and debriefed each of the *shelichim* in order to better understand the needs of the Russian group. Ultimately, in the course of seven years, Hirsch sent over four hundred *shelichim* to the Soviet Union. And, of course, he continued to visit himself. He and his wife, Linda, personally brought foodstuff, clothing, and medicine — items desperately needed in

R. to L. R' Essas, Ernie Hirsch, Moshe and Yana, of Moscow.

Moscow. His accomplishments were of the scope that would have made any large-scale organization proud, yet he did everything himself (and later, with the help of a few volunteer *yeshivah*-educated young men), right from his living room.

Rabbi Essas recognized his extraordinary efforts, and his first stop abroad after arriving in Israel was in Mr. Hirsch's London home. The Soviet Union, too, appears to have understood his unique contribution: On the third day of a visit in the summer of 1986, they knocked on Hirsch's hotel-room door. Hirsch was then roughly manhandled and interrogated. Finally, he was ordered to pack his bags and leave on the next plane out. The KGB had arranged — probably not accidentally — that this take place on Friday; thus, Hirsch barely had time to get home before *Shabbos*. He was one of the very few *shelichim* accorded this Soviet honor, and, perhaps, the only one in the *glasnost* era.

> *Some used to think that being a shaliach to Moscow was exciting, dramatic, the stuff spy novels were made of. Not really: mostly, it was a lot of hard work.*

◄§ A Week in Moscow

The bearded young man apprehensively boarded the Moscow-bound British Airways jet on Sunday afternoon. That evening, at about 6:00, he landed in Moscow's Sheremetyevo Airport. He anxiously awaited his

Ernie Hirsch and friends, reunited in Jerusalem, 1987. Code-name "Gingy" is third from right, second-row, in shirtsleeves.

luggage's arrival down the conveyor belt: After all, Ernie Hirsch had personally packed it the evening before, filling it with kosher food, *sefarim*, and, among other things, two pairs of *tefillin* (one pair, he would tell the authorities in case of trouble, was for the week; the other was for *Shabbos* use).

He cleared customs — he was lucky, and they didn't confiscate any of the food — and proceeded to make contact. The *shaliach* — let us call him Yoel — rifled through his wallet for a two-kopeck coin. Hirsch, with the foresight born of long experience, had made certain that he had a large supply for the local telephones: No calls were ever made from the hotel phones, which were almost certainly tapped.

Rabbi Essas' phone rang. "Hello, my name is Zevulun." When Rabbi Essas received a call from one of the twelve tribes, he knew it was one of Hirsch's men.

The meeting place was always the same: the first car of the subway train as it pulled into Sokol Station, near Rabbi Essas' apartment. It wasn't difficult to recognize the *shaliach*. Usually, he was the only one with a beard. Even the beardless, though, were noticeable among the old Russian *babushkas* and drunks who frequented the subway car. In any case, says Rabbi Essas, the *shaliach* always had a different look — his face would lack the tension that sixty years of KGB fear had imprinted on almost every Muscovite's features.

From Sokol Station they would carefully go to Rabbi Esssas' home.

A welcome visitor: R' Shlomo Noach Mandel of Toronto visits a Soviet family. The piles of diapers and linens on top of the closet were welcome gifts in the shortage-prone U.S.S.R.

The *shaliach* would spend hours in the cozy little kitchen, preparing a program for the week. Yoel was expected to give a *shiur* every night for a few dozen eager participants. (The *shiur* would be given in Hebrew; many of the English-speaking *yeshivah* students had to brush up!) During the day, from early morning to late afternoon, he would give classes to smaller groups, including several to groups of women.

As a *sofer*, Yoel had an extra duty: teaching several young men the laws and mechanics of *safrus*. At Rabbi Essas' request, Mr. Hirsch often sent *sofrim* and *shochtim* to help prepare the Soviet *ba'alei teshuvah*; in fact, several received *Kaballah* in *safrus* and *shechitah* right there in Moscow, under the tutelage of scores of differing *rebbeim*.

The week flew by, a kaleidoscope of classes, Torah learning, questions and answers. The next Monday would see Yoel safely back home. Within hours of his arrival, he was deep in conversation with Ernie

In the Essas apartment in Moscow, a sleepy family during a midnight briefing with a newly arrived shaliach.

Hirsch, giving him all the details of his trip, helping to plan the next *shaliach's* program.

> On occasion, the KGB played rough. Just to keep things
> interesting.

◆§ The Shaliach and the Secret Police

It began, as all foreign visits did, with a phone call. A code name, a time for a meeting. Not long afterwards, Rabbi Essas met a new friend in the station: Rabbi Shmuel Goldberg of Manchester, who came under the auspices of Ernie Hirsch to share his Torah knowledge with these thirsty Moscow Jews.

At first things seemed to go well, with absorbing, well-attended *shiurim*. Then, on Wednesday night, as he taught *Gemara* in a Moscow apartment to ten young men, came the sound of every *shaliach's* nightmare: a knock at the door.

The owner of the apartment walked carefully to the bolted door. "Who is it?" he asked quietly.

"Telegram," answered a brusque voice.

A telegram this late at night. Nonsense!

"Leave it by the door," the man said, trying to keep his voice steady.

"It must be hand-delivered," the man on the other side insisted.

"I cannot open the door now," the young Jew said. "I will pick it up at the post office."

There was the sound of retreating footsteps. The men looked at each other. Perhaps it had really been a postman? Maybe...

The sound of a door being angrily kicked broke the hopeful skein of their thoughts. Surely this was no conscientious postman! This was the KGB.

The men automatically went through the precautions they had been schooled in. The *Gemaras* were removed, cups of tea and plates of cake magically appeared on the table. And those most at risk — two university students — made their way to the kitchen to try and find a place to hide.

In the midst of all this controlled, frantic activity, Rabbi Goldberg sat, pale, wondering what the police would do when they discovered him here, a foreign citizen holding an unauthorized class in a forbidden religion.

The banging at the door continued relentlessly. Suddenly, four burly men jumped into the room — from the window. They had been in the apartment above and had actually climbed down a drainpipe to the balcony.

Without a word to the astonished group, they walked to the door to admit the policemen in the hallway. They then fanned out through the apartment, finding those who had hidden. (The university students were ultimately expelled.) Rabbi Goldberg was escorted to his hotel, and told that if he would meet anyone involved in anti-Soviet activities he would face charges.

Not until *Motza'ei Shabbos*, at the usual meeting place on Archipov Street, did a worried Eliyahu Essas find out the fate of his *shaliach*. As he stood in front of the Moscow Synagogue, he saw a familiar face: Rabbi Goldberg's. The Englishman managed to pass him by and mutter a few words, letting him know that he was fine.

Years later, in 1986, upon his first visit to England, Rabbi Essas was finally able to properly thank Rabbi Goldberg for the danger he had accepted upon himself in order to teach Torah.

Material assistance was an important element of the help from abroad. All foreign currency transactions were illegal, with penalties of up to ten years' imprisonment. Yet, tens of thousands of rubles were necessary to keep the camps going, to subsidize kosher food, to print sefarim, and to keep local authorities happy and quiescent.

The shelichim brought in a constant stream of saleable items to help fund the movement: Japanese cameras, sheepskin overcoats or even blank videocassettes. A network of brokers and middlemen were set up to sell these luxuries through government stores: though the brokers' fees were high, there was safety in intermediaries; even if someone got caught, the entire movement would not be endangered.

✍ Code Word: Baruch's Friend

The telephone rang shrilly in the Essas apartment. A voice on the other end said some meaningless pleasantries, then sent warm regards from "Baruch's friend."

"Baruch's friend": These were two words that meant much to Eliyahu Essas. They meant that Jews cared, that Jews from the outside were ready, as he and his friends were, to make sacrifices for their beliefs.

"Baruch's friend" was the code that meant a rendezvous with two very special men: Belgian businessmen Baruch and Yisrael Moshe.

Until he'd met these two men — one in 1973, in the Moscow Synagogue, and the other in 1979, through Rabbi Teitz — Essas had not had much contact with Jews who had come to the Soviet Union on legitimate business deals. Prominent businessmen would gladly offer donations to organizations that helped Soviet Jews, but few were willing to endanger their lucrative business deals by meeting with refuseniks, thus risking an encounter with Soviet authorities.

Baruch and Yisrael Moshe were two exceptional businessmen. And, more important, they were two exceptional Jews.

The moment they learned that there were Soviet Jews anxious to learn Torah, the two decided that they must help — despite the physical and financial dangers such help would entail. Swiftly, they organized an informal support organization of their own.

When the call came, when "Baruch's friend" was mentioned, Rabbi Essas knew that his friends had come. That night he stood at the corner of Karl Marx and Gorky. Behind him was the brooding shadow of the

Agudath Israel of America president Rabbi Moshe Sherer, Rabbi Essas, and Rabbi Mordechai Neustadt, head of Agudah's Va'ad L'Hatzolas Nidchei Yisrael, discuss ways of helping Rabbi Essas' brethren in the Soviet Union.

Kremlin and Lenin's Tomb. The wind howled, and the temperatures dropped to minus thirty-five degrees Fahrenheit. So much the better — there would be few people out here, braving the icy chill.

At precisely ten-thirty, a figure came out of the darkness, a bundled-up image carrying two heavy suitcases. A nod, a smile, a few cordial words, and the figure was gone — with only the suitcases remaining on the ground attesting to his presence.

Rabbi Essas took a quick look around him and picked up the luggage. Now came the really dangerous part. If a passing policeman would wonder what he was up to, if he would open up the luggage, there would be no question that Essas would wind up in jail, charged with black marketeering.

He looked around him for a cab. At last! He hailed the taxi and jumped in, grateful for the warmth and protection it offered. In a voice roughened by the cold, he gave his address.

Once at home, he opened the suitcases, and found a cornucopia of Jewish delights: pounds and pounds of kosher salami and hard cheeses, hand-picked *sefarim* that he'd requested the last time: *Pachad Yitzchak* and the *Machon Yerushalayim* commentaries on the Talmud; cameras

*R' Shlomo Eisen-
berger, a shaliach
from Telz, with
R' Essas.*

for resale; and toys and puzzles for the children studying in illegal classes.

"Baruch's friend" had come through again.

> In 1981, Rabbi Teitz brought the growing Torah network to the attention of Knessiah Gedolah of the World Agudath Israel, when he galvanized the international convention with tales of these brave young men and women who somehow accepted Torah under the Soviet regime.
>
> Almost immediately afterwards, Rabbi Mordechai Neustadt, head of Agudah's Va'ad L'Hatzolas Nidchei Yisrael, and activist Hershel Lieber made the trip and saw the miracle for themselves. Here were men learning Gemara — Gemara! — in the Kremlin's grim shadow.
>
> That was the beginning of Agudah's involvement in the Torah community in Moscow.

✐ Telz Tales

By the mid-1980s, when the man from Telzer Yeshivah traveled to the Soviet Union to visit his beleaguered brethren, the *shelichim* of Agudah and Ernie Hirsch were regular visitors, working in well-coordinated unity to bring material assistance, *sefarim* and *tashmishei kedushah*, and, most of all, their own learning to the avid group that so eagerly awaited their arrival. Virtually every week an Aeroflot, Pan American or British Airways flight would put down in Sheremetyevo Airport, bringing with it still another *shaliach*. Like clockwork they flew in, shared their Torah learning, and after a week, flew back to lands more hospitable to Torah Jews.

Until the man from Telzer Yeshivah arrived, and the clockwork went haywire.

An unexpected warm spell had turned Moscow's snowy streets into a river of cold, uninviting slush. But neither Rabbi Essas nor his visitor, the man from Telz, noticed their increasingly wet and cold feet. For the Telzer, this was both the beginning and the culmination of a dream: meeting the famed Soviet Rabbi who would serve as his guide and mentor, and at the same time as his student, for the next seven days; helping him to share his Torah knowledge with very special students.

For Rabbi Essas, although every *shaliach's* arrival was a special event, this visit promised a unique poignancy: This man was a Telzer. Rabbi Essas' mother had been born in the Lithuanian city of Telz; her grandfather had received his *semichah* from the *yeshivah* there. In a sense this tall, ramrod-straight stranger who studied in the "Telzer *derech*" had inherited the spiritual birthright that the Communists had stolen from him: They were brothers.

In his excitement, Rabbi Essas completely forgot to give his visitor the usual briefing — what *shiurim* to give, where to give them, what messages to bring to the outer world when he returned. Instead, the two men spent the night in rapt discussion of the Telzer *derech* of learning.

For Rabbi Essas, the rest of the week was a delightful dream. Like a KGB shadow, he followed the man from Telz everywhere, even to beginners' *shiurim*, reveling in uncovering his own spiritual heritage.

But alas, all dreams come to an end. The week was over, and it was time for the man from Telz to move on. For the next few days, until his departure, he was scheduled to visit Grisha Wasserman and bring his message of Torah and hope to the Jews of Leningrad.

The next day found the man from Telz wandering through the streets of Leningrad, searching through the rows of apartment buildings for the one that housed Grisha Wasserman.

He felt something amiss almost as soon as he began to climb the stairs. A silence that seemed somehow sinister filled him with foreboding. Another flight of stairs — and here before him stood four grim men, hats pulled low over their dark eyebrows.

The bewildered *shaliach* was hustled off into a waiting car and raced down to a police station. There, he underwent the classic foreigner's interrogation. *Who are you? What do you want here? What are you doing?* Again and again came the questions, unfailingly polite, dangerously unyielding.

As he had been instructed, the *shaliach* from Telz maintained a polite but indignant demeanor, and a resolve as unyielding as that of his interrogators. Outwardly, he answered no questions, but inside, his mind seethed with answers that would have stunned his foes. *Who are you?* A Jew who cares for other Jews, who cares enough to put himself in danger. *What do you want here?* I am trying to destroy your plans, as you have tried to destroy my people.

The hours passed, with Wasserman in Leningrad and Essas in Moscow waiting tensely for some word of their vanished friend. Finally, a contact brought them the joyous news: The man from Telz had been released with a warning to refrain from anti-Soviet activities.

To this day, no one is quite certain what triggered the KGB reaction — an overzealous bureaucrat or a reasoned decision to frighten away these intrusive foreigners. If it was the latter, it completely failed: With *sefarim* in their suitcases, and a prayer in their hearts, the *shelichim* kept up their vital work.

> *The man from Telz was not the only Agudah shaliach to come up against the formidable presence of the KGB. Rav Moshe Eisemann, mashgiach of Yeshivah Ner Yisrael in Baltimore and one of the few who made multiple trips to the Soviet Union, also came in for his share of unwanted attention. As he went through customs on one of his many trips to the Soviet Union, he was stopped by a stern official who took apart his luggage piece by piece, confiscating virtually everything he had brought for the network. He was then strictly warned to stay away from any illegal activities. Despite the danger, he insisted on remaining, though he did take precautions: never using the phone, never visiting Rabbi Essas in his home, and foregoing larger "public" shiurim for in-depth learning with a few advanced students.*
>
> *Most shelichim, though, had nothing to do with the KGB. Their encounters in Russia were very different — and much more pleasant.*

◄§ Ladies' Night

Mrs. Schwartz was nervous. Her husband, a *maggid shiur* in a New York *yeshivah*, had just left to give a class in Jewish philosophy to a group of interested Soviet Jews. She had remained behind in the Essas home to speak informally to several women who had recently returned to Jewish observance.

As she tried to settle the butterflies flip-flopping in her stomach, she remembered the words of the Agudah staff member who had briefed her before the journey. "These women need other women," he had said. "They need you to bring them *sheitlach*. They need you to teach them Torah. But, most of all, they need you to talk to them, to serve as a role model for a Torah-observant woman."

A role model? What could she teach these modern-day heroines, who had given up so much to observe the *mitzvos*? What in the world would she tell them? What would they think of her — a spoiled Jewish girl who had never made a single sacrifice for her religious beliefs?

She need not have worried. The eight women who came to meet her could not have been more gracious — or more excited to speak to their overseas visitor. Question followed question. Some of them, Mrs. Schwartz noticed, could have been asked in Manhattan as easily as in Moscow; others were unique to the Soviet Union. *How do I get my five-year-old to wear his tzitzis? How do I explain to him why he cannot wear his yarmulke in school? What do I do about milk and meat if I have only one sink? How can I be absolutely certain my wig looks natural? If my co-workers at the university realize I'm covering my hair, I may lose my job.* On and on, questions of Jewish daughters trying desperately to fashion lives and raise families without Jewish mothers to guide them.

> *What do you do when someone travels thousands of miles to come and bring you comfort and help — of a kind that you most definitely do not need?*

◄§ Shabbos Guests

The midnight knock on the door startled the sleeping Essas family into alert wakefulness. Could it be... was this the dreaded prelude to a KGB search?

No, the voices in the hallway were speaking English. Most definitely not the secret police. But who?

Rabbi Essas opened the door. By the flickering light of the candles he saw a sight that, if it was not as dreaded as the KGB, still meant trouble.

Foreigners wearing sheepish smiles — and no headcoverings.

This wasn't the first time that he'd been confronted by well-meaning emissaries of secular Jewish organizations. His name was on a list of refuseniks and occasionally they would call to offer assistance. He appreciated their sacrifice, accepted their gifts graciously — and gave their cans of *treife* beef soup and packages of non-kosher muenster cheese to non-Jewish activists, who heartily enjoyed them.

But tonight it was *Shabbos*. And here they were, smiling, speaking their accented American English, and expecting hospitality.

They had, they explained, called and called and called, but there had been no answer. And so they decided to just drop by.

How could he explain to these people, so dedicated to Jewish causes, who had come from the land of religious freedom, that he had not answered the phone because the Torah prohibited it, that they must now sit in the dim kitchen because turning on a light was one of the thirty-nine *melachos* of *Shabbos* — when they had never heard of the word, or concept, of *melachah*? How could he explain, without being insulting, that here in the Soviet Union he kept a forbidden Torah that their forefathers had discarded in a land of religious tolerance?

As best he could, careful not to be condescending or insulting, he explained that he was observant. They sat until two in the morning, talking amiably. And then it was time to go back to their hotel.

But how? There was no public transportation at this hour. Clearly, they expected Essas to help procure a taxi.

He walked out with them into the cold, rainy night. With a smile, he refused their offer to share an umbrella. Then, speaking in a lowered voice, he gave them their instructions. "You wait here. A taxi should pass soon. I will stay behind this tree, and will help you if you need it."

Doubtless, they thought that this was some sort of ploy to trick the guileful emissaries of the KGB. They never suspected that it was the guileless emissaries of some local Jewish federation who were being tricked, by someone who could teach Torah to professors of Moscow University, but who found it difficult to make secular Americans understand the Torah way of life.

"Mitzvah gorreres mitzvah: one good deed brings another in its train." Occasionally, one sees this with startling clarity.

⇜ Who's Helping Whom?

He turned up at Rabbi Essas' door one morning — an American tourist who had come to visit a refusenik. He found Rabbi Essas' name and address in his local Jewish paper.

What the young man — a doctoral student of theoretical physics at a North Carolina university — found, amazed him. He'd heard of Ilya Essas, a mathematician and activist who had been refused permission to leave the Soviet Union. What he found was a rabbi — a rabbi, for heaven's sakes! — a Talmudist, a practicing Orthodox Jew.

The sight startled and, perhaps, chagrined him somewhat. This Essas knew more about Judaism, had studied more Jewish books, here in the land of religious persecution, than he had in America, home of liberty and justice for all.

The two exchanged letters for a short time, but then, with his doctoral studies growing ever more arduous, the student ceased to write.

Three years passed. Rabbi Essas, involved in his multi-faceted activities, had forgotten about his young visitor from North Carolina. And then came a letter.

It was a wedding invitation from the young physicist, now working at prestigious Stanford University in California. Together with it, he had scrawled a short message. He was now an observant Jew, he told Rabbi Essas, marrying a nice Jewish girl.

He had not known how far that Aeroflot trip to Moscow would take him. His *mitzvah*, his concern for his fellow Jews, had surely led him to this new way of life.

CHAPTER 8

A Farewell to Russia

Prison. The word has a doleful, frightening sound: a place of felons, of wickedness, of the horror of freedom lost; the clanging of a gate slamming shut with an echoing finality; a room devoid of any semblance of humanity; coils of barbed wire pulsing with electric death for those who dare defy it.

For most of us in Western countries, the thought of prison is nightmarish, but one blessedly removed from our own daily existence. Not so for Soviet Jews. For many of them, each day was part of a sentence served, an interminable, open-ended sentence with scarcely the possibility of parole; the entire country was one vast prison cell. They were the men and women who had dared to defy the Communist authorities by asking to leave, the Jews who gave the lie to the myth of the Socialist paradise by demanding something better — the refuseniks.

Among the thousands of Soviet Jews denied exit visas to Israel was a family of five. The mother had worked for one year as an engineer in a factory that made missile launch pads. That was enough for the family's annual exit request to be denied, year after endless year, thirteen times in a row.

And so the Essas family waited...

◄§ Let This Family Go!

It was kind of a ritual in the Essas family: Each year they would renew their request for an exit visa at the local OVIR office; each year they would again be refused.

Now it was 1979. Rabbi Essas had already begun teaching Torah, creating the *talmidim* who would help him build a network of observant Jews in this most atheistic of cities. And his name, heretofore only appearing on some bureaucratic lists, was beginning to get noticed.

1979 was the year Rabbi Aharon Rakefet, a student of Rav Y.B. Soloveitchik and a noted Torah lecturer from Jerusalem, was sent by the Israeli Foreign Ministry, under the guise of an American businessman, to contact various leaders of the refuseniks. When he saw the *shiurim* that Essas had organized right under the nose of the KGB, he was impressed. Very impressed. Impressed enough to create the Committee to Free Eliyahu Essas — complete with logo and stationery. Never mind that the committee consisted only of Rabbi Rakefet and his wife. Like Essas himself, Rabbi Rakefet was determined to prove that, with unceasing efforts and a large dose of *siyata d'Shmaya*, anything could happen. And often did...

> As part of his efforts on behalf of the Essas family, Rabbi Rakefet got in touch with Rabbi Moshe Sherer, president of Agudath Israel of America. Rabbi Sherer put his own considerable political expertise into play, conducting high-level talks with Congressmen and the White House in attempts to get an exit visa for the Essases.
>
> At the same time, the untiring Rabbi Rakefet brought the Essas case to the notice of the World Jewish Congress and its Secretary-General.

◄§ *The Elusive Mr. Singer*

In the clandestine world of refuseniks, there was a constant networking going on, continual messages being passed from one to the other: Go to this man, he can help you. Try that one out, he has political influence. Check out so-and-so — he has friends in the media.

So when the name Singer was mentioned as a good contact, Eliyahu Essas looked up in interest.

Dr. Israel Singer, his contact said. Try to get in touch with him. He might be of use to you.

Dr. Israel Singer. Essas envisioned him: a doctor or academic, one with good political connections.

Before he could find out how to make contact with Dr. Singer, Essas heard of another possibility. Rabbi Yisrael Singer, someone told him, was a man he should get to know.

Rabbi Yisrael Singer. The name had a nice ring to it. Probably someone who could help out with the *shiurim*, and possibly with getting the *tashmishei kedushah* that were so desperately needed by his growing network.

Singer? You want to talk to Singer? That must be Mr. Singer, the Jewish organization man. An important fellow to meet with.

By now, Rabbi Essas was getting confused. Singer the Rabbi, Singer the academic, Singer the top executive of a secular Jewish organization. How many Singers were there, anyway?

Only one, he soon found out. In 1984, during his weekly vigil in front of the Moscow Synagogue on *Motza'ei Shabbos*, Essas was introduced to Yisrael Singer, Secretary-General of the World Jewish Congress, and an observant Jew: a man equally at home in the boardroom and the *beis medrash*; a man who was soon to dedicate an enormous amount of his time to the cause of getting Rabbi Essas out of the Soviet Union.

Over the next four years, Singer and Essas met many times, usually in deserted Moscow parks in the middle of the night, often in freezing weather. Rabbi Essas particularly remembers one horribly cold night when they plodded through a thick combination of snow, rain and mud that stuck to their boots. *This should keep the KGB away*, he said to himself. *And at the very least*, he thought, as the viscous, gooey mess made its way through the top of his boots and settled coldly at his frozen toes, *if they are watching, they'll be as uncomfortable as we are!*

Singer put Essas' name on the top of the World Jewish Congress list of refuseniks. In addition, he introduced Essas to still another important contact — WJC president and international business tycoon, Edgar Bronfman.

For some Russians, a slug or two of vodka is enough to bring happiness. But the refuseniks wanted more than a bottle of schnapps: They wanted the man who bottled it!

◄§ Stolichnaya and the Synagogue

The Moscow Synagogue was in an uproar. What could possibly be happening? On this everyday morning — not *Shabbos*, not a festival — instead of the usual ten or fifteen elderly Jews, there were about seventy

26 MARCH 1979

LEONID BREZNEV
PRESIDENT OF THE UNION OF THE SOVIET SOCIALIST REPUBLIC
THE KREMLIN
MOSCOW
USSR

MR PRESIDENT

I APPEAL TO YOU IN THE CASE OF MY SON ILYA ESSAS TOG
WITH HIS WIFE ANYA AND MY THREE GRANDCHILDREN JOSE'
AND DAVID ALL OF WHOM LIVE AT CHASOVAYA STREET 26

SINCE 1973 MY SON AND HIS FAMILY HAVE REPEATEDLY
PERMISSION TO EMIGRATE TO ISRAEL AS IS THEIR HEA

NEITHER MY WIFE NOR I HAVE SEEN OUR ONLY SON OR
SINCE WE EMIGRATED TO ISRAEL THREE YEARS AGO.
NEVER SEEN OUR LATEST GRANDCHILD BORN FIVE MON

REFUSAL TO ALLOW OUR IMMEDIATE FAMILY TO BE F
AGAINST THE SPIRIT OF BOTH THE U N DECLERATI
AND THE HELSINSKI AGREEMENT. ON A PERSONAL N
(THE INTERNATIONAL YEAR OF THE CHILD', I AS
AND TO GRANT EXIT VISAS TO MY SON, DAUGHTER
GRANDCHILDREN.

SIGNED

TZVI ESSAS
C/O 10 REDINGTON ROAD
LONDON N W 3
ENGLAND

52/32 REHOV MOSHE SHARRET
KIRYIAT SHARRET
HOLON

Honorable Edward M. Kennedy
109 Russell Senate Office Building
Washington, D.C. 20510

September 1

Dear Ted:

It was a special delight meeting you again in Washington a
dinner in honor of Prime Minister Begin at the National Portrait
as now sitting to ask you to place special emphasis on a partic
a Russian Jewish "refusenik": Ilya Essas, a 35-year-old Russia
has been trying to leave for Israel since 1973. He is married t
engineer, Anya, and the Russian government turned down their requ
exit visa on the grounds that Anya's work for one year in 1970 ir
office was classified. (Anya's superior in her job was permitted
that very year.)

During the last few years that the Russians consistently reje
applications for exit to Israel, Ilya Essas became an Orthodox Jew
and an outstanding expert in traditional Jewish literature. He ha
primary influence on a large number of Jewish families in Moscow w
turned to their Jewish faith because of his teachings.

Ilya is the only child of his parents, who reside in Israel si
His parents are literally heartbroken, and it would be a deed of gr
to reunite his grieving parents with their only son, daughter-in-la
grandchildren. Ilya, who has given so much of his brain and heart a
help others during the past decade in Moscow, really deserves this s
kindness.

Ilya Essas has become a worldwide symbol, a heroic person who un
difficult circumstances was able to reach such outstanding heights of
scholarship and educational activity in the constricting atmosphere o
You will earn the gratitude of Jews throughout our country if you can
him by making a personal intervention on his behalf with the Russian a

Warm regards.

Sincerely,

Rabbi Morris Sherer
President

: Ilya and Anya Essas, Chas-

GERALD R. FORD

April 29, 1985

Dear Ambassador Dobrynin:

I write to urge that Ilya Essas obtain permiss
emigrate from the Soviet Union and most since
hope that such permission will be granted.

As I understand it, Ilya Essas has sought an e
visa for sometime without success. As you kno
a number of members of the Congress and other
ranking government officials have urged that a
ative action be taken. I can assure you that a
favorable permission would be widely appreciat
in the United States.

It was a real pleasure to participate with you
the Conference in Atlanta and it was most enjoy
to renew our long friendship. Any assistance i
this matter on behalf of Ilya Essas I would gre
appreciate.

Very best wishes from Mrs. Ford and me.

Sincerely,

His Excellency Anatoly F. Dobrynin
The Ambassador of the Union of Soviet
   Socialist Republics
1125 Sixteenth Street
Washington, D.C. 20036

Посольство
Союза Советских
Социалистических Республик

"18" August, 19

13, Kensington Palace Gardens
London, W. 5
Tel: BAY 3628, 8629

Re: Ilya Essas and family in Moscow

Thank you for your letter of 4 Ju
I advise you that the USSR Embass
does not have any information with re
question you touch upon.
   Permit me to assure you that as
received any details of the subject y
in, they will be forwarded to you imm

Yours sincerely,

Ministe
Embassy

Let my son go: Letters written on behalf of refusenik Ilya Essas, together with a hard-to believe plea of ignorance by the Soviet ambassador

BENJAMIN A. GILMAN
22ND DISTRICT, NEW YORK

COMMITTEE
FOREIGN AFFAIRS
SUBCOMMITTEE
INTERNATIONAL OPERATIONS
ASIAN AND PACIFIC AFFAIRS
CHAIRMAN
TASK FORCE ON
AMERICAN PRISONERS AND
MISSING IN SOUTHEAST
ASIA

Congress of the United States
House of Representatives
Washington, D.C. 20515

COMMITTEES
POST OFFICE AND CIVIL SERVICE
SUBCOMMITTEES
INVESTIGATIONS
HUMAN RESOURCES
SELECT COMMITTEE ON
NARCOTICS ABUSE AND
CONTROL
RANKING MINORITY MEMBER

June 14, 1983

Mr. Yuri Andropov
Secretary General C.P.S.U.
The Kremlin
Moscow RSFSR
USSR

Dear Mr. Secretary:

We are writing you in behalf of Ilya Essas and his family, residents of Chasovaya Street 26 in Moscow, and strongly urge that you allow them to emigrate to Israel.

Ilya Essas has been denied an emigration permit for a decade, despite the fact that his wife Anya has not worked in her capacity as an acoustical engineer for over twelve years. Their applications to emigrate have been repeatedly denied on these now outdated grounds.

Mr. and Mrs. Tzvi Essas, parents of Ilya Essas, were allowed to emigrate to Israel in 1976, and have not seen their only child since. Furthermore, they have never even met the youngest of their three grandchildren, David, now five years old.

In the interests of family unity, we, as Members of Congress, appeal to you to grant emigration visas to the Essas family. Tzvi Essas, at 73 years of age, has said, "I am not going to live much longer. I want my son and his family with me. We suffer, my wife and I, we long for our son."

We urge you, on humanitarian grounds, to allow the entire Essas family to be reunited. As a signatory to the Helsinki Final Act, we urge you to comply with the guarantees for family reunification called for in that agreement.

Sincerely,

CHRISTOPHER H. SMITH, M.C.

BENJAMIN A. GILMAN, M.C.

NORMAN F. LENT, M.C.

JOSEPH P. ADDABBO, M.C.

BILL GREEN, M.C.

HAMILTON FISH, JR., M.C.

JAMES WEAVER, M.C.

GARY L. ACKERMAN, M.C.

RAYMOND J. McGRATH, M.C.

HOWARD L. BERMAN, M.C.

PATRICIA SCHROEDER, M.C.

MAJOR R. OWENS, M.C.

MICHAEL A. ANDREWS, M.C.

TOM LANTOS, M.C.

DALE E. KILDEE, M.C.

WILLIAM J. HUGHES, M.C.

LES AuCOIN, M.C.

JAMES J. FLORIO, M.C.

DANIEL B. CRANE, M.C.

MICKEY LELAND, M.C.

MEL LEVINE, M.C.

BILL FRENZEL, M.C.

ROBERT G. TORRICELLI, M.C.

MARTIN FROST, M.C.

L. to r. Rabbi Singer, Edgar Bronfman, Rabbi Essas, at a closed executive meeting of the WJC in Jerusalem, 1986.

young people in attendance, praying the *Shacharis* service! Unheard of!

The elders of the synagogue looked at each other nervously. Suddenly, they heard the roar of an automobile. Someone ran outside to see what was happening, and then returned, panting and almost trembling in excitement. The word got around — a Chaika! Someone had arrived in a Chaika.

The elderly men nodded soberly. First, this huge crowd; now, a Chaika — the limousines given out only to important government officials or VIPs. This boded no good, whatever it was.

At the end of *Shacharis*, that young upstart, Eliyahu Essas, rose and approached the *bimah*. With a respectful nod to the elderly men, who looked at him stony faced and suspicious, and a pleasant smile to the young men — all of them his *talmidim* — he proceeded to introduce the mystery man of the Chaika — Edgar Bronfman.

The Canadian billionaire, heir to the Seagrams' fortune and president of the World Jewish Congress, then got up and addressed the group. "You are not alone," he said. "World Jewry stands with you, fighting for the right of every Soviet Jew to have a Jewish education and emigrate to Israel."

This speech of Bronfman's was more than an inspiring talk to a group of Soviet Jews — it was his way of publicly raising the ante in a four-year-old game that he was playing with the Soviet authorities.

In the currency-hungry world of the Soviet economy, Edgar Bronfman was a man who counted. A Canadian billionaire, a major player in multi-national firms such as Dupont, Texaco, and, of course,

Rabbi Sherer and Rabbi Essas.

his own Seagrams, he was a figure to be courted, feted, and royally treated.

But Bronfman was more than a billionaire. He was head of the WJC and, in that capacity, he wanted to help his fellow Jews.

For four years, the Soviet government had issued formal invitations to Edgar Bronfman, Chairman of the Board of Seagrams. For four years, the invitations had been accepted, graciously, on WJC letterhead. His Soviet hosts had talked business; he had talked visas. They had talked about deals; he had talked about people.

And now, with this speech, arranged without the prior knowledge of the government, Bronfman was making a statement. I am interested in Jews, he was proclaiming, even more than Stolichnaya vodka.

The efforts of so many — Rabbi Rakefet, Rabbi Sherer, Yisrael Singer and the WJC, Edgar Bronfman, along with the countless western Jews who wrote letters, sent telegrams, joined demonstrations, and said endless "kapitlach" Tehillim — finally seemed to bear fruit. The end approached. But slowly, so slowly...

December 1985. A dark, cold Moscow night. A resident at Pravda Street looked out the window to see if the wet, unforgiving rain was letting up at all. Suddenly, his eyes grew wide. He rubbed them and gave himself a shake. Was he dreaming? Was that a huge car, bigger than any car had a right to be, pulling up right in front of his house?

A uniformed chauffeur leaped out of the front and effortlessly swung the doors of the stretch limousine open. Regally, with the confidence of power radiating from him, Edgar Bronfman stepped out of the warmth of the car — and slid straight down into the thick Moscow mud. Ignoring the muck that greedily enveloped his Brooks Brothers custom-designed suit, the Canadian billionaire, the man whose name regularly appeared on Fortune Magazine's list of the ten wealthiest men in North America, made his way up the dimly lit staircase to give Eliyahu Essas a message.

"We shall meet in Jerusalem," he told Essas. "Very soon."

Though heartened by the billionaire's confident declaration, Rabbi Essas was by no means sanguine about his chances of obtaining his long-sought-after freedom. After all, it had been only four months ago, in September of 1985, that Yisrael Singer had told him in the Moscow Synagogue that a high-placed Foreign Ministry official had promised that the WJC's top three refuseniks — Ida Nudel, Iosef Begun, and Essas — would be freed shortly. At the time, Singer had promised to call him before he left Moscow that evening, hopefully with good news. But no good news had been forthcoming.

About one week after Bronfman's evening visit, as Rabbi Essas stood teaching in front of a group of young people, his host suddenly interrupted the *shiur* with a message for the Rabbi. "Telephone call. Important. Your wife."

Rabbi Essas rushed to the phone, his heart pounding. In all the years that he had been teaching, his wife had never once interrupted a lecture. What could have happened? The children —

His wife's voice, reassuringly quiet though tinged with excitement, calmed his fears. "OVIR has just contacted us. We must come down immediately to claim our exit visas."

Exit visas! Freedom!

Rabbi Essas looked at the faces of his *talmidim*, expectant, radiant with Torah knowledge. He had waited thirteen long years for the privilege of getting this visa — thirteen years of teaching, of learning, of hoping and praying.

He turned back to the telephone. "I must finish my *shiur* here. You go pick them up for us."

After taking thirteen years to make up its mind as to whether or not the Essas family could leave its borders, the Soviet government now gave them seven days to wind up their affairs, pack their suitcases, and say goodbye to their friends, relatives, neighbors and *talmidim*. In those mad, hectic hours of pain and joy, Mrs. Essas took care of all the packing, the endless documentation, the selling and giving away of furniture and household effects, the purchasing of tickets (Rabbi Essas had put the rubles for tickets in a special bank account years before, in the hope that someday it would be needed). Rabbi Essas spent the week seeing student after student, meeting representatives from his city and others, trying to ensure that his network of Torah study and observance would continue without a break, even after he was gone.

Neighbors who had gotten used to the sight of Chaikas, stretch limousines, and KGB Volgas pulling up at their door watched on that Tuesday morning as two taxis pulled up. Nine people — Rabbi Essas, his wife and three children, his wife's parents, and two relatives — piled in. With the slam of a door, a roar of a motor, they were off on a route they'd dreamed of for more than a decade — the Leningrad Highway to Sheremetyevo International Airport.

At the airport, they found more than fifty of Rabbi Essas' *talmidim* waiting to say goodbye to their *Rebbi*. There were hugs, kisses, messages to relatives, whispered prayers. The Soviet government, too, had its own special goodbye for the Essas menage: Its customs officials tore apart much of his luggage, and even ripped the lining of Essas' jacket in a futile search for illegal currency.

In Vienna, the Essas family was greeted by representatives of the Jewish Agency, Rabbi Mordechai Neustadt of Agudath Israel's Vaad L'Hatzolas Nidchei Yisroel, and by their two friends from Antwerp, Baruch and Yisrael Moshe. Another friend, Shlomo Goldschmidt of Zurich (whose son, Rabbi Pinchas Goldschmidt, now serves as Av Beis Din in Moscow), accompanied the family on the El Al jet that was to bring them to their final destination.

On the flight, Essas sat near an Israeli absorbed in his Hebrew-language newspaper. The man, hearing Essas speaking in Russian, then spoke. "It says here that a big Russian rabbi is coming to Israel," he said casually. "I wonder if you know who he is."

From Moscow to the Marriott: Not long after emigration, Rabbi Essas receives Agudath Israel's Netzach Yisrael Award at the National Convention. L. to r. R' Chaskel Besser, vice-president; R' Essas; R' Mordechai Neustadt; R' Moshe Sherer.

Encounter in Bnei Brak. R' Essas, R' Shlomo Lorincz, Rav Eliezer Shach shlita.

In the news: Rabbi Essas meets with political personalities in his efforts on behalf of Soviet Jews.

מזכיר המדינה השווייצרי נפגש עם הרב אסאס
בביקור במלון "זילברהורן" היהודי בגרינדלוולד

לא בכל יום מבקש מזכיר מדינה להתארח במלון יהודי ולעמוד מקרוב על ייחודו של מלון שכזה. עוד פחות סביר שזה יקרה בשווייץ, ארץ יקרה המשופעת במלונות פאר, ודווקא שם זה קרה. בעיצומו של קיץ כאשר תיירים יהודים רבים, מכל קצווי תבל, גדשו את מלון "זילברהורן" שבגרינדלוולד הגיע פניה מלשכתו של שר המדינה ושר החוץ בפועל, אדוארד ברונר, עם בקשה לארגן לשר ביקור במקום. בעלי המלון, מאיר וורות וגנר שמכירים את עומק העבודה של השר הפופולרי הופתעו לשמוע כי הוא מבקש להגיע למלון כבר למחרת. כאשר הוא הגיע לא הרגיש בהפתעה. הכל היה ערוך ומוכן. קבלת הפנים היתה מרהיבה, כמו בביקור רשמי של אישיות ממלכתית עליה שוקדים חודשים מראש.

הדחיפות בארגון הביקור נבעה מ...

<!-- clipped newspaper photos with partial headlines -->
הגיע מסורב העליה

חזקים, אבל בלי חוצ...

אליהו אליה אסס מתי...
מאת חן ארקין
"זו יציאת מצרים
צלי וכבר בשדה -"

הרב אליהו אסס, מסורב־עליה, שנת מאבק על זכותו לצאת מ־ שמעון פרס ואמר לו: ישראל צריכה להיות חזקה, אבל אל־לה לנהל מדיניות חוצפנית או גזענית.
(כתב: רוני שקד, צילום: זום 77)

של הרב אליהו אחי...
למען יהדי...

למסורב העליה אליה אסאס

נפל התשופה בן גוריון, 22
(תאי"ם) "זו יציאת מצרים שלי" אמר בבואו לישראל אמש אליהו (אליה) אסאס, מסורב צליה שחזר בתשובה אחרי מלחמת ששת הימים וכאו קיים חיים יהודים דתם בוטחטה ונאבק על זכותם לגצא לישראל.

אסאס בא יחד עם אשתו אניה וסלושת ילדיה הקטנים והתאחד נתחברות רבה הם הוריו, צבי וסונגרו אסאס מחולון שעלו ליש־ ראל ב־1976. בעונה קבלת פנים לצליה החדש נראתה כמה שזור כמעש ולא נראה צליה בנמל התעופה. מאות פעילי העליה וחברים כילאו את מסע העליה הע־ נבל, ודר הפנים הרב פרץ הע־ נבל, היו בין ה...

לתחמפיקאי במקרצור, אסאס, בן 40, הי זה הרבה ליד וילנה, 21 שנים במוסקנה, יסאו שביקש ל־ צלות לישראל היה נתן לתחירות את ולצבצת אך לא נצצר אף פעם. סירוב השלטונות להתיר לו ול־ אשתו רעות לישראל הוסבה בכך שאסאה, מהנדסת עבדה במצל דצ־סודי. עם חזרו בתשובה גיהל ממלטית שם היתה לה ניחה למי־ דע סודי. עם חזרו בתשובה ניהל דרס הברית חיים דתיים אדוקים, למד עברית, הבין ילדיו לבר־ לצניינג' הלכה, בתקיום בכל ה־ מצוה והרחיב ידיעותיו בכל ה־ נוגע ליימודי קודש, הפלשח ב־ ניתקו השלטונות את קשרי לדי־ ביתו פעמים אחדות, החרימו ספרי־ תו וזרזו בה חיפש, הזהירו או־ קודש וספרים אחרים, תי לא יקיים כמוצ על המצוה ...
ב־1976 אך כאמור הוא לא נוצר.

Rabbi Essas, too excited to want to engage in lengthy explanations and conversation, just smiled.

Later, when the El Al Boeing 727 had finally landed, the Israeli watched as government representatives and media photographers met his erstwhile seatmate. He rushed over to him. "Why, you're the Rabbi I was reading about! Can I have your autograph?"

But he was too late. Rabbi Essas hardly heard him. He was off, racing towards the door, racing towards *Eretz Yisrael*.

CHAPTER 9

Postscripts: A New World

The Chafetz Chaim, it is said, gave Communist hegemony just seventy years before its complete downfall. His words have proven almost hauntingly prophetic: Just about seven decades since the October Revolution, the Soviet Union and the Communist Party that ruled it ceased to exist.

It began with a new leader, a hard-faced man who, with his KGB background, seemed to be still another dictator. But Mikhail Gorbachev spoke differently than his predecessors. He spoke of glasnost and perestroika and of opening his benighted country to the West. And he meant what he said.

The years since Gorbachev attained power brought with them privatization, coups, Yeltsin, independence movements. And, finally, the U.S.S.R. ceased to be, replaced by the Commonwealth of Independent States.

And while this newest Russian Revolution has been going on, the Jews have looked for one thing: freedom to leave, freedom to make aliyah to their own land.

With hundreds of thousands of Jews from the CIS now emigrating to Israel, the story of a religious revival has changed radically. Gone are the perils of the KGB; today, those at the forefront of the movement to teach Torah to Soviet Jews fight, instead, an atheism ground deeply into a people, together with complete ignorance of many things Jewish. Former Soviet Jews are allowed to learn Torah and fulfill mitzvos — but will they want to?

Today, there are many organizations and institutions in Israel and countries throughout the world that have opened their doors to the new immigrants, hoping to teach them that being Jewish means more than having the word Yevrei written on an identity card. Among those working tirelessly with his brethren is Rabbi Essas, who, in his capacity as head of Ohr Somayach's Russian-language program for young men, is, once again, teaching Torah and creating talmidim.

The stories of the Russian immigrants and their newly found Torah learning are many. What follows is but a small sampling.

◄§ Dima Becomes Dovid

Dima was born in Rostov, a large city in Russia located on the River Don, in 1969. His childhood was typical of many Russian Jews — a grandfather who drank wine on Friday night without knowing why, a pervasive atmosphere of atheism in school, a vague dissatisfaction with the Soviet system and an even more nebulous feeling of Zionism in the home. His mother, afraid for him, refused to allow her infant son to be circumcised.

Dima was a bright boy, who did well in school. He particularly remembers one biology lesson, when he was about twelve years old. His teacher explained to the class that mankind had descended from the ape family.

Dima, puzzled, raised an inquiring hand. "If this is so, why don't we see monkeys today turning into men?" he asked.

The teacher smiled at his innocence. "Life is different today," he explained. And that was that.

But Dima remained puzzled and unsatisfied.

Dima had hoped to go to college, but because of some blatant anti-Semitism on the part of the school administration, he didn't get in. Instead, he served for two years in the Soviet army. It was here, in this unlikely milieu, that the notion of emigration first came into his head.

To supplement his scanty rations — more often than not, Dima and his fellow soldiers supped on bread and soup only — Dima planted a small vegetable garden near his barracks, carefully tending the potatoes, cucumbers, and tomatoes. He bought a chicken and enjoyed fresh eggs; he raised rabbits for meat.

A sergeant who passed his "farm" one day looked at Dima and grinned. "What are you doing here, fool?" he asked. "You should be farming in Israel!"

Ohr Somayach students enjoy a "tiyul" in their new homeland.

It was the first time he had ever thought of it.

In 1990, Dima's aunt kissed her family goodbye and left for Israel. In 1991, his great-grandmother, age 93, followed. (Though many said she wouldn't survive the trip, she insisted that she preferred dying en route to Israel than staying behind.) When Dima's army stint ended, he decided that he, too, would make the move.

Though he had been in a classified position, and normally would have been told he had to wait five years for a visa, somehow he got permission after just seven months. Thus, in April 1991, Dima of Rostov found himself with a relative in the lovely port city of Haifa.

To make up for the abysmal lack of knowledge of most immigrants, Dima's *ulpan* included classes in Jewish history and holidays. In the heat of the summer, he carelessly flipped open a pamphlet in Russian that his teacher had given him. It spoke of an unknown holiday called *Tishah B'Av*.

Dima read through it, interested. Someone had written tellingly of a Temple's destruction and how Jews the world over mourned for it. He was particularly struck by the story of Napoleon, who saw in the Jewish mourning the sign of their eternity.

Dima went back to the title page and read the name of the author: Rabbi Eliyahu Essas.

R' Essas lecturing in Ohr Somayach.

But though the pamphlet and classes spurred Dima on to attend twice-weekly lectures in Judaism, he was much too busy making a life in Israel to give serious thought to Jewish observance. With the *ulpan's* end, he planned on taking the entrance exams for Haifa's Technion University. Here, at least, no one would deny him entrance because he was a Jew.

Dima spent the weekend before the exams with friends in Haifa. On the table, he saw a Russian-language newspaper published in Israel. Though he normally did not subscribe to or even read it, he felt impelled to pick it up and skim through it.

His eyes were drawn to a small advertisement. Young Soviet immigrants were invited to apply for a special program in Jerusalem that combined university level studies with classes in Judaism. The program led to a degree in either computers or business, and classes were available in Jewish history, Talmud and Torah. The name of the institution sponsoring the program was Ohr Somayach.

It sounded intriguing, very intriguing. The only problem was, he was in Haifa, the program was in Jerusalem — and exams were only days away!

Dima decided to take a quick trip to the capital city to check out the program. He was taken to the office of the director for an interview.

Sitting behind the desk was a Rabbi — Rabbi Eliyahu Essas, the man who had written the pamphlet that had so interested him.

He would go to one *shiur* to see what it was all about, he decided. Again, it was Rabbi Essas who stood before him.

"*Bereishis bara Elokim,*" the rabbi intoned, beginning a class in *Chumash*. "G-d created the world."

Someone asked a question. How old is the world that G-d created?

The answer was forthcoming, and quickly. Five thousand seven hundred fifty-one years ago, G-d created the earth.

Suddenly, Dima was transported to another time, another place. He was twelve years old again, and he wanted to know why monkeys did not turn into men.

And now, at last, he was getting his answers.

After seven months Dima — now Dovid — began learning *Bava Metzia*. He found it perplexing, challenging, frustrating — and the most rewarding study he had ever done. A year after his arrival in the program, he was reveling in "*nafka minas*" and making enormous progress.

Only one thing marred Dovid's satisfaction and happiness. His mother and two younger siblings were still in Russia.

During a trip sponsored by the *yeshivah* to *mekomos kedoshim* in *Eretz Yisrael*, Dovid found himself at Miron, praying at the graveside of Rabbi Shimon Bar Yochai. He remembered his *Rebbi's* words a few days earlier, when he had confided to him his longing for his family to join him. Rabbi Essas had spoken of the power of prayer, and had counseled him never to give up hope and to continue to *daven*.

He *davened* in Miron, and then at the grave of Rabbi Yonasan ben Uziel in Amukah, with all the fervor he could muster: Please, let them come join me here.

Two days after his return to *yeshivah* he received a telegram from Moscow. His family was on their way to Israel.

ᴥ§ A Delayed Return

Michoel began to study Hebrew while still living in Riga. In the late 1980s, with perestroika the new reality, learning about his Jewishness was not much of a problem. Riga Jewry, after all, had only come under Communist hegemony in the 1940s, and many of the older generation had clear memories of Jewish life. In fact, a plethora of old organizations

A Soviet immigrant celebrates his chasunah in Ohr Somayach, Jerusalem.

had sprung up anew, revitalized: Betar, HaShomer HaTzair, and the like.

Michoel had undoubtedly never heard of Yisro, but in a sense he followed the path of that seeker of truth, checking out the different organizations and the philosophies that underlay them, searching for the "ism" that would lend his Jewishness true meaning and fill a void in his life and his soul.

Among the many people whom Michoel met in his search was one Arthur Uritzky, a *ba'al teshuvah* and member of Moscow's Torah network living in Riga. Michoel attended a few of Arthur's classes, spoke to him several times — and then faded out of the picture.

As it did for so many Soviet Jews, the scene then shifted from Russia to Jerusalem. Uritzky, who now gave *shiurim* and served as a dorm counselor in Ohr Somayach's Russian-language program, got a phone call. A voice from the past. Michoel's voice.

He was calling from a kibbutz. He had met a *shaliach* from the kibbutz while still in Riga, and upon his *aliyah* had gone to visit him, to study life on a kibbutz.

He had tried Communism while still in Russia — and rejected it. Secular Zionism, as practiced by his Riga fellows, was also not his way. Now he had seen the peculiar amalgam of socialism and Zionism that the kibbutzim had created — and still, the void was not filled. Now the only thing left to search out was. . . Torah.

The choice, if clear, was not easy, and for a time Michoel vacillated, living on a kibbutz while frequently appearing, Afro hair and all, on Uritzky's Jerusalem doorstep. He visited a *shul* for the first time and saw, to his astonishment, the unity of Jews all answering *"amen"* at the same time. He sat in on *shiurim*, checked out *yeshivos*. And, finally, enrolled in one.

Today, Michoel lives is a small religious suburb of Yerushalayim, a *shomer Shabbos* Jew whose Yisro-like search has finally had its happy ending.

When he received his long-awaited visa and boarded the plane to Eretz Yisrael, Rabbi Essas' joy was tempered by the knowledge that he left so many of his brethren behind, men and women whom he would have wanted to speak to and teach. As an Israeli citizen, he would be completely cut off from Soviet life, exiled from the land of his birth forever.

Forever, in this case, lasted all of three years.

~§ Return to Moscow

The year was 1989. The place was Moscow. The event was the International Book Fair.

Among the Israeli delegates to the massive fair was an intense, bearded man who, unlike most of the others, spoke a fluent Russian. His name? Eliyahu Essas.

In his role as a tourist, Rabbi Essas was able to make contact with the *talmidim* he had left behind, and savor the heady, though strange, sensation of being a *shaliach*, a visitor instead of one of the visited.

During the course of his visit, Rabbi Essas met Leib Gelfman, a middle-aged prominent broadcasting personality who was head of a regional capital's television station. They had talked for a few moments

In Yerushalayim at last: Rabbi Essas, the Belzer Rebbe, Mr. Chaim Bronner of Antwerp.

about emigration. A Jew's home is in Israel, Rabbi Essas told him firmly. Then the man went on his way.

Three years later, the telephone rang in the Essas apartment. The man on the other end spoke Russian; nothing unusual in this unofficial home and center for Soviet emigres. What was unusual were his first words to Rabbi Essas. "In Moscow, you told me that a Jew's home is in Israel. Now, I am here."

Rabbi Essas paused for a moment, then smiled. "What took you so long?" he asked. "We've been waiting for you."

> This man, through his connections with Rabbi Essas, ultimately found more than a homeland — he reclaimed his lost heritage. He and his wife now attend Torah classes at various institutions in Jerusalem, and his children are learning in yeshivos, the oldest son studying in Ohr Somayach. The whole family became observant Jews.
>
> "We've been waiting for you." The Jewish people has been waiting for the Mikhails, the Sergeis, the Alexeis and Anyas and Natashas; for the Jews of Moscow and Riga, Odessa and Bukhara.
>
> And slowly, ever so slowly, we have been watching them come back to their home — and their Torah.

R' Essas, R' Eisemann, and R' Yaakov Yitzchak Ruderman zt''l (Rosh Yeshivah Ner Israel), discuss the Moscow teshuvah movement, 1986.

Future mothers: Neve Yerushalayim's Russian-language-program graduates, 1991. Anya Essas (second row, fourth from left) heads the program.

And what of that very unusual Russian immigrant, Rabbi Eliyahu Essas? For thirteen long years he had dreamed of joining his brethren in Eretz Yisrael. What happened once he finally arrived, once the first euphoria had died down and he was forced, like all immigrants, to make a new life in a very new place?

Oddly enough, Rabbi Essas' life did not change as radically as one might have thought. In Moscow, Eliyahu Essas had taught Torah. In Jerusalem, too, he taught Torah. In the Soviet Union, he had dedicated his life to spreading Yiddishkeit; so too in Israel.

With the continued help of the WJC, and the understanding of Rabbi Israel Singer and the WJC head in Israel, Dr. Avi Bekker, Rabbi Essas immediately flung himself into the job of speaking out on behalf of Soviet Jews trapped behind the Iron Curtain; and once the Curtain had been flung open, reaching his brethren in Israel. Combining his own knowledge and experience with the visionary approach of Rabbis Mendel Weinbach and Nota Schiller of Yeshivah Ohr Somayach, and Rabbi Dovid Refson of Neve Yerushalayim Seminary for Girls, Rabbi Essas worked to formulate a program that would teach young Soviet Jews all the knowledge that their homeland had denied them.

The past years have brought, of course, their share of frustrations, and more than their share of rewards. Rabbi Essas himself best describes the challenges and joys of those years: "When they come to Israel, these young men and women have no more Yiddishkeit than they had in the USSR. Nature abhors a vacuum: They had filled themselves with all sorts of non-Jewish ideas and philosophies. It is our obligation and our challenge to help them find their roots, and plant them in the land of Israel, so that the entire Jewish people can be proud of the fruits of our labors.

"Programs such as that of Ohr Somayach and Neve Yerushalayim are almost the only way possible to give eternal meaning to the revolution that began in the USSR. We are not talking about a small group of friends — we are talking about the entire Jewish people. When we see young men and women who barely know the aleph-beis, with no idea of their common past or heritage, who can, after a year of study, live proudly as Jews in the land of their forefathers Avraham, Yitzchak, and Yaakov — then we see the revolution that began in Moscow continuing on. And we are all a part of that unstoppable stream."

Appendix

For close to two decades, Rabbi Eliyahu Essas has been teaching Torah. In Moscow and Jerusalem, to five people and five hundred, underground and publicly, he has been working in *kiruv rechokim* with astounding success.

The first key to this success is, of course, an enormous helping of *siyata d'Shmaya*, without which the most carefully prepared lesson will fall on deaf ears.

In addition, Rabbi Essas has made himself five firm rules, culled from years of experience, which he finds are necessary to success in teaching Torah to those who know little or nothing of it.

Here, for the benefit of those who have ever tried to reach out to their fellow Jews, are Rabbi Essas' five rules of *kiruv*:

1. Everything must be honest. The world is a complex place, people aren't angels, life is not always black and white. Even religious life and people are not always perfect. Don't whitewash, don't conceal difficult truths. Not everything must be said — but whatever is said must be true. Soviet Jews, particularly, have not been schooled in trust of authority: Too much of what they have heard has come out of the Communist propaganda mills. Do not play a role, do not pretend to be a representative of an ideal world. Be honest, and earn the trust of *talmidim*.

2. Avoid confrontations. Invite the prospective *talmid* into the laboratory of your thoughts and feelings. Share his questions, show them how you have reached your answers and conclusions. Don't simply state something as a given; be prepared to understand and allay his doubts and questions.

3. Show your *talmid* that being a Torah Jew is the normal way of life. Don't preach: "You must do this; you must do that." Show your

talmid that if he wants to live a Jewish life, this is what he should be doing. Try not to prove anything, just let him see that this is simply normal Jewish behavior.

4. Never discuss Hashem's existence. The student will see that you believe in G-d; don't try to prove anything to him. Just show the depth and beauty of Torah thought, and the Torah explanation of the world and humanity. From this beginning, the person will naturally gravitate to the author of Torah, the Creator of the universe.

5. The means of bringing a Jew back to Torah is rooted in *ahavas Yisrael*. We must feel vast respect and love for our fellow Jews, never looking upon them as inferiors. Don't put on airs — I know something you don't know. Let them see your happiness in being a Torah Jew — and let them understand your wish for them to attain that same spiritual satisfaction.

This volume is part of
THE ARTSCROLL SERIES®
an ongoing project of
translations, commentaries and expositions
on Scripture, Mishnah, Talmud, Halachah,
liturgy, histroy, the classic Rabbinic writings,
biographies, and thought.

For a brochure of current publications
visit your local Hebrew bookseller
or contact the publisher:

Mesorah Publications, ltd

4401 Second Avenue
Brooklyn, New York 11232
(718) 921-9000